How to Audition
for the Musical Theatre

A Step-by-Step Guide to Effective Preparation
Revised Edition

HOW TO AUDITION FOR THE

THEATRE

A STEP-BY-STEP GUIDE
TO EFFECTIVE PREPARATION

Revised Edition

Donald Oliver

A Career Development Book

SK
A Smith and Kraus Book

A Smith and Kraus Book
Published by Smith and Kraus, Inc.
One Main Street, PO Box 127, Lyme, NH 03768

Copyright ©1985 by Donald Oliver; ©1988, First Revised Edition; ©1995, Second Revised Edition. First published by Drama Book Publishers, New York.

Manufactured in the United States of America
Cover and Text Design by Julia Hill
Cover illustration entitled "The Singers Audition" by Al Hirschfeld © Al Hirschfeld. Drawing reproduced by special arrangement with Hirschfeld's exclusive representative, The Margo Feiden Galleries Ltd. New York.

First Edition: September 1995
10 9 8 7 6 5 4 3 2 1

Library of Congress Cataloging-in-Publication Data

Oliver, Donald.
        How to audition for musical theatre : a stip-by-step guide to effective preparation / by Donald Oliver. -- Rev. Ed.
        p. cm. -- (A career development book)
        Rev. ed. of : How to audition for the musical theatre. Rev. ed. 1988.
        ISBN 1-880399-58-X
        1. Singing--Auditions. 2. Musicals--Auditions. I. Oliver, Donald. How
                to audition for musical theatre. II. Series.
        MT892.04 1995
        792.6'028--dc20   95-22917
                                                            CIP

ACKNOWLEDGEMENTS

Both as a professional and personal colleague, director Bill Gile played an important role in my developing many of the ideas in this book. So I take this opportunity to thank him, not only for all the times he hired me as an audition accompanist, which allowed these theories to develop, but also for his advice and opinions as this manuscript took shape. I was also fortunate to have received guidance early on from the extraordinary pianist and composer Sande Campbell. She was also gracious enough to contribute a few more thoughts for this revised edition and I am in her debt.

I am also deeply appreciative of all the people who took the time to share their helpful ideas and audition stories: Jeanie Breall, Mary Jo Catlett, Joseph Church, Martin Connor, Jeffrey Dunn, Rob Fisher, Paul Ford, Scott Frankel, Paul Gemignani, Sheldon Harnick, Jerry Herman, Peter Howard, Jeffrey Huard, Julie Hughes, John Kander, Barry Kleinbort, Jack Lee, Larry Moore, Barry Moss, Richard Northcutt, Norman Rothstein, David Spencer, Eric Stern, Edward Strauss, and Susan Stroman. Sadly, certain people whose comments and recommendations are freely incorporated into the text passed away since they generously spoke with me. I most sincerely thank the late Morton DaCosta, James Kirkwood, and Peter Wandel. I miss them all terribly.

No practitioner of the arts can survive
without a nurturing environment.
I am blessed with a large, warm, wise, loving,
and unshakably supportive family.
It is to all of them that I dedicate this book;
but most especially to my parents,
Abraham and Rhoda Oliver,
to my aunt, Rosalind Oliver,
and to the memory of Bernard Oliver,
my beloved uncle.

CONTENTS

ACKNOWLEDGEMENTS V

THE "IF-YOU-SAW-THIS-SCENE-IN-A-MOVIE-YOU-
WOULDN'T-BELIEVE-IT-FOR-A-MOMENT" DEPARTMENT 1

INTRODUCTION: THE GROUND RULES 3

ALL ABOUT AUDITIONS 7
    The Production Team   *11*
    The Interactive Elements of an Audition   *13*

GETTING YOUR FOOT IN THE DOOR 21
    How to Arrange an Audition   *22*
        Public Announcements   *22*
        Agents   *26*
        Casting Directors   *26*

PREPARATION PART I: SELECTING MATERIAL

WHERE TO FIND AN ACCOMPANIST 31

YOUR AUDITION REPERTOIRE 32
    Building a Song Portfolio   *33*

WHAT NOT TO SING 40

WHERE TO FIND SONGS 49

PREPARATION PART II: THE MECHANICS

HOW TO PREPARE YOUR MUSIC 57
    Transposition   *58*
    Professional Copying   *60*
    The Care and Feeding of Your Music   *62*
    Taping Your Music   *64*

INTERPRETATION: ACTING THE SONG 66

WORKING WITH A VOCAL COACH 71

PERFORMING

WHEN TO BRING YOUR OWN PIANIST 77
    Advice to the Personal Accompanist   *80*

SINGING THE RIGHT KIND OF SONG 81
    Rock Musicals   *82*

AT THE AUDITION: DO'S AND DON'T'S,
HINTS AND SECRETS 85
    Excuses, Excuses, Excuses   *94*

HOW TO TALK TO THE PIANIST AND WHAT TO SAY 98

WHAT TO DO IF YOU FORGET THE LYRICS 101

THE OPEN CALL 102

SUMMER STOCK 105

AT THE CALLBACK 107

A TOUCH OF THE OUTRAGEOUS......................... 109

AFTER THE AUDITION................................ 112

APPENDIX

APPENDIX A: A Partial List of the Most
           Overdone Uninspired, (and Inappropriate)
           Audition Songs...................................... 116

APPENDIX B: Your Photo and Résumé 120

APPENDIX C: To Agent or Not to Agent 123

APPENDIX D: Helpful Names and Addresses 128

ONE LAST AUDITION STORY 139

ABOUT THE AUTHOR 141

HOW TO AUDITION FOR THE

Musical

THEATRE

A STEP-BY-STEP GUIDE
TO EFFECTIVE PREPARATION

The "If-You-Saw-This-Scene-In-A-Movie-You-Wouldn't-Believe-It-For-A-Moment" Department

THE TIME: Recently.
THE PLACE: New York City.

A replacement was needed for the supporting role of Tess in the Broadway production of the Tony-award-winning musical, *Crazy For You.* On an appointed day, twelve hopefuls sang and danced for the powers-that-be. Then five of the original twelve were asked to stay and read.

The Director was not totally pleased with any of the candidates. The production team knew they were working against the clock—they had to get somebody in the show quickly. What to do? Should they settle for one of these ladies or should they somehow try to find someone else? (They already felt as if they had seen everyone in the city who was even remotely right.) Then the Casting Director said there was one other possibility, a woman who was not in town that day, but who could come in to audition the following day. The Director decided to postpone making a final decision until he saw this mystery girl. His co-creators thought it would be a real longshot for someone to be so much better than anyone they had just seen to warrant another day of auditions.

But in a sincere effort to find the best possible Tess the production team reassembled the following day after the matinee performance at the theatre where *Crazy For You* was playing. Out came the woman to audition. She was tall; that was a plus for this role. Hmm. The Choreographer's assistant put her through her paces in the dance combination. She could tap well enough, and made the Choreographer confident that the woman could be taught the show's dance routines. But could she sing? Yes she could sing, and she even sang a comedy song, which made the Director especially take notice. The team thought that this was too good to be true. She looked right, she could sing and she could dance. Nah, she'll never be able to read. Well when she read the excerpted dialogue she was really, really funny. The Director took a bit of time to work with her on her acting. Then the Stage Manager appeared and announced that in precisely five minutes he would have to begin the pre-set for the evening's performance no matter what, so they had to finish up. The Director asked the woman to wait while the staff huddled together in the audience to talk over the situation.

The woman stood alone on the stage of the Shubert Theatre, one of the most famous and beautiful theaters on Broadway, and waited while her future was being decided for her. Finally, the Director stood up and called out to her, "You're hired!" At that very instant the pre-set began: the front stage lights lit up bathing the girl in light, and the stagehands pulled in the show's spectacular finale set pieces (a fantasy-land of gold and silver staircases) around her. She squatted down and started to cry. The Stage Manager reappeared and took her down to the costume department. She started rehearsing the very next day.

Introduction: The Ground Rules

Can you remember the moment you first decided to pursue a career in the musical theatre? Was it when you had a solo in a school show and heard the audience applaud you for the first time? Was it when your favorite relative heard you sing? Saw you dance? Said you were every bit as good as anyone already on the New York stage? Or did you get bitten when you saw a certain movie or live show—perhaps a touring company—and afterwards exited the theatre exhilarated? Did you proclaim to anyone who would listen, "That's what I want to do!"

Well, congratulations! You have picked a field that is every bit as glamorous as it is simultaneously demanding, competitive, ruthless, and frustrating. Always remember that show business is a *business,* filled with myths and misconceptions, legends and lore. Anyone who pursues a career in "Show Biz" is in for a rough ride.

Within this most changeable and unreliable of professions there is only one constant: a staggering rate of unemployment (at any given time over 95 percent!) In the early stages of their careers, almost all performers are forced to work at decidedly unglamorous jobs in order to support themselves. Many wait tables or clean strangers' apartments. And all the while they wait for, in the words of the late writer/actor James Kirkwood, "a committee composed of Agent, Producer, Casting Director, Director, Writer—and sometimes even a star or two"—to agree that they are— "right for a part," thus allowing them to work at their chosen profession.

This is not only true of up-and-coming performers; at most stages of your theatrical career you will not have much, if any, power in deciding when you can ply your trade. So it is vitally important to always stay focused and do positive things to help your career's forward progress.

As Oscar Hammerstein II wrote in the song "Happy Talk" from *South Pacific:*
You got to have a dream—
If you don't have a dream
How you gonna have a dream come true?
If you want to make *your* dream come true, you'll do whatever is necessary to make it happen. Sensibly. To the very best of your abilities. And the first step is learning how to master the one thing over which you have complete control: how you get yourself ready to face that decision-making committee.

You have in your hands a manual on how to prepare for a musical audition. This book is a primer on how to present yourself and your talent in the best possible light at the audition itself.

During the first thirteen years of my (somewhat checkered) career in the professional New York theatre I played the piano for literally thousands of auditions. It always amazed me how many talented people made similar mistakes while auditioning, diminishing their chances of being seriously considered, while some performers with less natural ability made the absolute most of their potential—and got the jobs.

From analyzing all that I witnessed, I came to the somewhat less-than-earth-shattering conclusion that if you have your act together, it is possible to weight auditions in your favor by minimizing your risks.

This book will lay out the proper guidelines. Although geared primarily for people new to the business, it should be helpful to performers at any stage of their career. If an actor or actress is just starting out, following the advice herein can make him or her seem to be a seasoned professional at their very first audition. Those experienced at auditioning will find much useful information, especially if they are constantly auditioning and not getting jobs. As you will see, there's usually a reason for that, and the solution to the problem can be found between these covers.

The assumption with how-to books is that once read and absorbed, mastery of the subject discussed and imminent success are inevitable. Look closely at the title of this book; it is not called *How to Get Cast in a Show*. I couldn't make that kind of promise. But there is a methodical way of approaching an audition. The procedures proposed in the following pages come from experience. Most are founded on some very simple principles that can be put to use immediately—at your next audition.

There are three things to bring to your attention before we begin.

First: Despite my natural irreverence I do understand the importance in being politically correct in the times in which we live. At least in print. But in order to prevent the awkwardness caused by trying to avoid sexist terminology—see earlier in this preface—I will employ the time-honored tradition of masculine usage throughout the text. Unless specifically indicated, all remarks and advice are meant for both men and women. And if in the course of the text I refer to a woman as a "girl" please don't write to the publisher to complain. I'm not being sexist or demeaning; I'm just trying to vary the vocabulary.

Second: In discussing the audition techniques in the pages that follow, I mention for the purposes of illustration many specific songs. They are discussed here based only on their appropriateness as audition material. My singling them out is neither meant to imply any personal opinions on their inherent merits—or demerits—as songs, nor to imply any negative criticism of their suitability in their original dramatic contexts. And at no time is it my intention to show disrespect to the songs' creators.

Third: All the stories in this book are absolutely, cross-my-heart true, including the magical tale which begins this book. Honestly. I couldn't have made up the shenanigans you'll read about. If you recognize an error of your own in one of these stories, don't whip yourself—just pay attention to how to correct your mistakes. Quoting an oft-used line, anyone claiming resemblance to anyone described should be ashamed to admit it.

If you are like me and are always looking for a shortcut, read no further. Here it is: You can distill everything in this book down to one important word—

> a word for which there is no substitute;
>
> a word that if taken to heart will make a huge difference in your
> career;
>
> that magic word is *preparation*.

This book will show you how to prepare effectively for almost any kind of musical audition you are ever likely to encounter. Although all of the examples and audition stories use the New York professional arena as their setting, the basics are the same whether you are auditioning for an end-of-season summer-camp production, a lodge pageant, a college show, or the latest $8 million Broadway extravaganza.

Please read this book carefully.
Prepare.
Break a leg.

All About Auditions

Since you have this idea that you'd like to perform in public someday, you'll have to let those people who can make your dream come true know you're alive and kicking. You'll have to attend auditions.

An audition is an event at which performers desirous of being part of a production demonstrate their talents to the people who will make casting decisions. First the auditioner will sing. Then, if his singing is found acceptable, he may be asked to read a scene from the show aloud, possibly in tandem with someone else auditioning the same day. Most probably he will read with a Stage Manager, or some neutral person hired by the production.

If the membership of Actors' Equity (the union for theatrical stage performers) were polled, you would find that the vast majority really don't like auditioning. Many people quit acting because they couldn't deal with auditions! Well you know what? The people who must evaluate auditions don't much like the process either. But so far no one has found a more effective system for viewing and assessing talent.

The process of auditioning has numerous drawbacks. For one, actors are performing without costumes, makeup, or proper lighting—hardly optimal circumstances.

And, for two, most are nervous. No, wait a minute, maybe "nervous" is too gentle a word. Most people are probably petrified of auditioning.

With good reason. An audition is the show-business version of a job interview. In a very short amount of time, actors have to perform a mini-commercial, and the product they are hawking is themselves. One young man was so rattled at his audition that as he was singing the song "Oklahoma!," he spelled it, "O-K-L-M-N..."

A lovely and talented singer-actress I worked with confided to me she conquered her panic over auditioning by thinking of each audition as a performance. She said that if she adds up all the auditions she does in a year, it amounts to quite a lot of performing time. So in her own way, she psyched herself to the point where she actually looks forward to auditioning.

Many actors suffer from lack of confidence in their abilities. This, combined with nerves, adds up to an insurmountable combination. The open call for the Broadway show, *The Happy Time*, was the first New York audition for one young man. He watched as the other actors arrived and changed into their jazz shoes and tights; he immediately felt out of place because he didn't have any special "rehearsal" clothing, just his tennis shoes and jeans. After many others were eliminated because they were physically wrong for the show, he was among those who were asked to stay and dance. First came a jazz combination; several guys were dismissed, he stayed. Then came the ballet combination; again, to his surprise, he was among those who remained. The Director/Choreographer of the show, the late Gower Champion, who was sitting nearby on a folding chair, came up to the young man and asked, "Have you had any formal dance training?" The young man answered, "A little, in college." Mr. Champion asked, "Are you a singer?" The young man replied, "I sing a little; I'm basically a dancer-actor." Mr. Champion said "I want to do something with you later when I get finished, so please wait over here" (indicating the side of the stage). The audition continued, the dance combinations got harder and harder, and more and more people were eliminated. The young man watched, sweat pouring down his body, feeling more and more inadequate as time went on. Finally, he could not take the (internal) pressure any longer, and he bolted. Only much later did he find out that *The Happy Time* had a role for which he was suitable: it was mainly an acting role, whose singing and dancing requirements were modest. The role was ultimately cast from those who attended that open call.

It doesn't help anyone's level of discomfort to realize that an audition can represent only one of several appearances before those doing the hiring. Casting their show is a serious enterprise for the creative team, so they reserve the right to have you audition for them on more than one occasion. These return visits are termed "callbacks." (Many years ago there was virtually no limit to the number of times you could be called back for a Broadway show without compensation. Actors' Equity, the union for stage performers, now restricts the number to 4 auditions for principal performers and 3 auditions for chorus members (without compensation). After these limits have been reached and the production still wants you to return for another audition/callback, they must pay you.)

The excitement of being called back for a second or third hearing doesn't make actors any less anxious than they were the first time. The pressure increases as the stakes become higher.

Everyone—including any star you can name—had to audition at one time or another in his career.

Barbra Streisand auditioned for Eddie Blum of the Rodgers and Hammerstein casting office when *The Sound of Music* was on Broadway. She was hoping to take over the featured role of Liesl—who sings "Sixteen Going on Seventeen." To impress Mr. Blum, she sang for three hours. Afterwards, Mr. Blum gave her much encouragement but told her she wasn't right for anything in *The Sound of Music.* The lucky one here was Mr. Blum, who was the recipient of a free, private, three-hour Barbra Streisand concert.

Even a performer as gifted as John Travolta had to learn the basics of auditioning. While performing in an Off-Broadway production of *Rain,* a nonmusical play, he was asked to audition for the prestigious Goodspeed Opera House in Connecticut. According to witnesses, he apparently hadn't been previously coached in the mechanics of a musical audition. Not being prepared to sing with a live pianist, he brought a cassette recorder with him—his musical accompaniment was on tape—and when he sang, he was not quite in sync with the recording. Extremely jittery, he made a bad showing and couldn't convince the producer of his potential worth. Now at that time, he was merely one of many performers who auditioned for Goodspeed and didn't make it. But he didn't let it discourage him; he kept at it and learned what he didn't know. Soon thereafter he landed important roles in the Broadway shows *Grease* and *Over Here!*, which led directly to the first phase of his exciting television and movie career.

Is it clear by now that it takes guts to audition? I hope so. Here are three more stories that tell about star performers with guts; coincidentally, each story has to do with a different musical whose score was written by Jerry Herman. Remember as you read—at the time these incidents took place, none of the three shows mentioned were the celebrated, wildly successful, award-winning musicals we now know them to be.

Carol Channing has been a bona fide star since 1949 when she played Lorelei Lee in *Gentlemen Prefer Blondes* and introduced the song "Diamonds Are A Girl's Best Friend." In 1963 she had to audition for *Hello, Dolly!* Why? Because the role of Dolly was a departure for her from Lorelei Lee and the other kinds of roles she had been previously associated with. She was neither offended nor afraid—she knew what she had to offer, and she understood that the production team needed to be convinced she had the particular quality they were looking for. She went on to win the 1964 Tony Award for Best Actress in a Musical. Just for the record, her competition that year was none other than Barbra Streisand in *Funny Girl*, Beatrice Lillie in *High Spirits*, and Inga Swenson in *110 in the Shade*.

In 1965, when the musical *Mame* was looking for its leading lady, Angela Lansbury had already been nominated for three Academy Awards. Every major female star at that time was either considered for or approached to play Mame. Everyone from Judy Garland to Ethel Merman to Mary Martin. Everyone but Angela Lansbury. Ms. Lansbury, who had starred in the musical *Anyone Can Whistle* on Broadway the year before, came to New York on her own and auditioned. But on the day of her audition the only one of *Mame's* creators she impressed was its composer/lyricist, Jerry Herman. Afterwards, without the knowledge of the producers or Director, Mr. Herman secretly taught her "If He Walked Into My Life," the stunning song from the score, and arranged for a second audition at which he played the piano, accompanying her. We all know now about Ms. Lansbury's subsequent triumph in the show, but at the time it was very brave on her part to go along with the second audition, because it could've gone the other way. She too, as did Ms. Channing, won a Tony Award, beating out Gwen Verdon in *Sweet Charity,* Julie Harris in *Skyscraper,* and Barbara Harris in *On A Clear Day You Can See Forever.*

La Cage aux Folles was a show for which auditions for the stars were mandatory. The requirements for the leading roles were so unique that the previous work of any actor wasn't enough to show the creators exactly what they needed for their leads. George Hearn was a much respected, hard working, versatile actor with an off-stage reputation as an accomplished lothario, who, prior to 1983, never even fantasized about dressing in women's clothing. But he wanted to play the role of Albin in *La Cage,* and with absolutely no guarantees that it would turn out favorably, he had the courage to agree to have Ted Azar—*La Cage's* talented hair and makeup designer—help him get completely done up in female attire for his audition. In drag, Mr. Hearn marched onto the stage, sang "My Heart Belongs To Daddy," and the part was his. He showed the production team that he had the theatrical guts they needed for *La Cage.* When he accepted his Tony Award, he pointed to it and said, "What some people won't do…"

THE PRODUCTION TEAM

For a moment, let's look at things from the point of view of those casting the show.

The creative team has to see and seriously consider sometimes up to 100 people a day for several days in a row. They have to impartially compare the relative abilities of everyone who auditions, trying to remember who was good, who was not, who should be seen again for the current production, and who may be useful in the future.

This is neither an easy nor an enviable task. The minutes spent watching that certain percentage of auditioners whose talent is not readily discernible add up to a valuable chunk of time most creative people could use doing other important preproduction work. And an astonishing number of talented performers are ill-prepared to audition, in ways which are fully described in this book. Their allotted moments in front of the people they're supposed to impress is a waste of time for both parties. For example, on the way to her audition, a girl stopped at a store and bought the sheet music for "I Cain't Say No." She told the staff pianist to begin at the chorus. He did. She sang the words of "I Cain't Say No" to the tune of another song (by the same writers), "I Enjoy Being a Girl." She got through the first four lines and sensed something was wrong. She asked to restart. The second time proved to be merely a repeat of the same problem. She restarted yet again. Same problem; and she still couldn't figure out what was wrong. The Director said "Thank you. That's what we need." And the poor girl left the room totally perplexed.

While they are planning (or envisioning) the production, the creative team usually has a pretty good idea of what they're looking for in their future cast members. If they are even the slightest bit uncertain about the ideal physical look of the characters, they know the fairly inflexible (and in some cases pretty well impossible) technical requirements for the roles. When you stand before the casting team they long for you to be the answer to their prayers because they can relax only when someone appears who is perfect for their needs.

In a conversation with me, composer John Kander (*Cabaret, Chicago, Kiss of the Spider Woman*) underscored the fact that the people judging an audition really do want you to be good when you step out in front of them because they have to cast all the roles in the show—except, sometimes, the star parts—from the people who audition. Jerry Herman said, "We're really nice guys who want to hire everybody. It's painful to see talented people walk by and not be able to use them."

The late Director Morton DaCosta (*Auntie Mame, The Music Man*) told me that at auditions he suffered as much as the people auditioning. Having first been an actor—most Directors and Choreographers started out as performers—he knew firsthand what the actors go through.

Because of the stakes, the members of the creative team are often just as nervous and apprehensive as you are. Mr. Kander tells of an incident during the casting of his show *The Happy Time*, when someone auditioning had an unusually large nose. The late Gower Champion, who directed and choreographed the show, was well known for his kindness and consideration during his auditions. Mr. Champion and the authors felt so sorry for this particular performer that, although pressed for time, they allowed a complete song to be sung and were overly solicitous afterward. In an ill-fated attempt at graciousness, Mr. Champion jumped out of his seat in the theater and rushed up onto the stage where he said, "Thank you, that was very nose."

THE INTERACTIVE ELEMENTS OF AN AUDITION

As the production team considers you, the following elements dynamically interplay:

1. YOUR "LOOK" AND YOUR "TYPE"

The first consideration is how close you are to the Author's or Director's physical concept of the role. In the musical theatre, because of time limitations (and the ratio of dialogue to songs) characters are written in very broad strokes. Each major role serves a plot function which can usually be placed in a specific "category": The Leading Man, The Leading Lady, The Villain, The Comic Best Friend, etc. If the Director casts someone who is the physical embodiment of the essence of the character, the audience readily accepts the actor in the role.

So to use a simplistic example, if they're set on a blonde and you're a brunette, you probably have very little chance of changing their minds. Don't tell me that you can wear a wig. The rigors of the audition process for the creative team don't often allow much time for imaginative thinking. I don't mean to take away your hope, and I said that this was a particularly simplistic example. Auditioning is an interactive process and your strengths in any of the other areas talked about later can make a difference if your physical "type" does not strike the team immediately.

One of the very first things to do is to HONESTLY figure out what category or type you naturally fall into. Are you the "handsome, young, leading man" or "beautiful leading lady" type? Or does your face and figure suggest a "character" type? Do you look your age? Younger? Older? Can you vary your look to expand your suitable age range?

You must be ruthless about any positive changes you are able to affect in your appearance to get cast in the type of roles you want. For example, if you are overweight and perceive yourself as the leading man or leading lady type, you'd be well advised to shed the extra poundage immediately. Think about it: How frequently do you see an obviously chubby hero or heroine in the theatre or films? Not often. And even then, how often is the lead's chubbiness not an integral part of the story?

In England, an adult man not more than four feet tall was being seen for a "panto" (a Christmas-time entertainment in Britain, usually a humorous re-telling of a fairy tale with fantasy elements). He entered the audition room and stayed a few minutes. Suddenly he came back out into the waiting area looking furious and slammed the door behind him. "What happened? Didn't you get the part?" asked one of his fellow auditioners. "Yes, I got the part." he answered. "Another &*^&*#% dwarf part!!"

Being a specific type isn't at all a bad thing. People have had wonderful careers playing the same kind of part over and over. Yes, I realize that being "typecast" isn't the most ideal situation ultimately; actors like to stretch themselves and all that. But this book isn't about how to combat that problem. It's about auditioning and getting acting jobs. If you are aware of where best you fit in the theatrical landscape, and are able to do what you do very well, you'll always work.

2. YOUR VOICE

This category concerns the quality of your vocal instrument and your range. If you are a lyric soprano and the score doesn't call for that, you could have the most magnificent voice ever heard on earth and still not get a callback.

I urge women to develop a "chest voice" as well as a "head voice" —with proper training both techniques can be used without hurting your throat. Never forget the golden rule of auditioning: the more versatile you are, the greater are your chances.

This may come as a surprise, but you don't have to be a phenomenal singer to get cast in a musical. If you register well in most of the other areas mentioned in this section, your voice might be "good enough" for the purposes of the show. As will be discussed at length later, you must carefully select songs to sing that show off your voice —whatever your ability—to maximum advantage.

3. YOUR ACTING ABILITY

More on this later in the book. (See Interpretation: Acting the Song.) In brief, having a glorious voice is not enough. You must have something going on behind your eyes. You can't just sing your song; you must act it as well and you will never get hired for speaking roles if you can't act. In addition to your voice training, you should be attending acting classes and/or scene study workshops. When you open your mouth to sing, people can tell immediately whether or not you can act your way out of that proverbial paper bag.

4. YOUR DANCE ABILITY

The days when all shows had separate singing and dancing choruses are long since over. Economic realities made this so. Nowadays, although some productions may require a "soloist" dancer (who does not have to sing well—or at all) or a singer with vocal needs so specific as to make their lack of dancing skills a non-issue, the creative personnel on almost all shows want to hire performers who can "do it all." This is especially true when casting a new show, whose requirements are likely to change during the rehearsal/tryout period. So all actors are counseled to be as well equipped with the tools of their trade as possible, to make it possible for them to be cast under the widest variety of circumstances.

If you are not a dancer and never will be, you still need to learn how to "move." (You will often see casting notices in the trades for "singers who move" or "singers who move well.") To accomplish this, Tony-award-winning Choreographer Susan Stroman (*Crazy For You, ShowBoat, Big*) strongly suggests that you "take some movement classes just to help you learn dance combinations at auditions. You don't have to take a 'dance' class; you could take a 'soft-shoe' or any kind of 'beginner' class. It is just to get you in the habit of picking up choreography. A lot of people lose jobs because they can't pick up the combination fast enough. In the fifteen minutes allotted to teaching the combination at an audition they have to either learn it quickly, or show that they can learn it; that spending time teaching them during rehearsals would be productive. People without any sort of training often have trouble learning even the easiest walking combination."

Of course, if you have the drive or the inclination, you should go ahead and take dance classes on a regular basis, whether it be ballet, jazz, or tap. Dance training gives you an awareness of and confidence in your body, in the way you move, and in the way you look to others. One-line parts in shows—such as, "Telegram for you, Sir,"—are almost always given to dancers rather than to singers simply because dancers are more certain to look graceful crossing the stage. Dance classes are relatively inexpensive—they cost a lot less than vocal coaching—and, at least in New York City, there are so many different classes taking place each day, it's easy to find one at a convenient time.

True, to land a lead in a show you don't have to be as proficient as a chorus gypsy; but if you are called upon to execute a few dance steps as part of your song routine, you won't look graceful without training.

Here's the theatrical golden rule again (in other words): You can never be too talented—or too skilled. You must be as versatile as possible. The competition is too stiff.

5. YOUR CHOICE OF MATERIAL

A large section of this book is devoted to helping you choose the right material to audition with. Briefly, just as the proper choice of a song can perk up the ears of the listeners and make them react favorably to your talent, the wrong choice can adversely affect your "castability." The casting team writes down what songs you sing, and later, when the inevitable discussion takes place as to whether or not you should be given a callback, you are often remembered chiefly by what song you sang.

6. YOUR APPEARANCE

Although being in show business grants people the right to a certain flamboyance, you should *always* come to an audition dressed conservatively. Be well groomed with a sensible, as in not-too-trendy, haircut.

MEN: A jacket and tie is the safest way to go except during hot weather when a clean sport shirt will suffice.

WOMEN: Dress as if you are going to a really nice cocktail party. The best outfit is a skirt or dress that is flattering, feminine, and comfortable. A woman should look like a woman; even if there is 13" of snow outside you should take off your snow boots, change from your ski pants, and put on a skirt and heels and look pretty. A little glamour couldn't hurt, but avoid overdressing; don't wear hats, gloves or excessive jewelry.

I realize there are other clothing choices for both men and women that would serve nicely. Obviously I can't opine on every possibility, so I am talking about safe, all-purpose dressing.

If you have specific knowledge of the show for which you are auditioning you may want to choose your clothes by taking into account the show's setting, allowing you to be seen in the appropriate context. Try to capture the essence of the show without coming in costume. Examples:

> • If you are auditioning for *How To Succeed In Business Without Really Trying,* which takes place in a white-collar corporate world, do not show up dressed as a cowboy. Gentlemen might wear a three-piece suit.

- If you are auditioning for a production of *Les Misérables* or *Fiddler on the Roof,* looking vaguely "peasanty" is better than showing up in smart, tailored clothing (i.e. no three-piece suit).

- If you're auditioning for a rock 'n roll show, look like a rocker. Not to an extreme, but you can dress a little funky.

And now a few words about footwear, ladies first. Please wear attractive shoes which help you move gracefully. Platform or "wedgy" shoes are cumbersome and ungainly. Open-toed shoes where your toes hang out over the front lip are not very attractive. Bedroom slippers, no matter how comfortable, are best left under the bed. Buy one good pair of fashionable shoes in a neutral color which can go with many different outfits and only wear them as your "audition shoes." As for the men, although I've seen sneakers and boots look both stylish and flattering, they may not be appropriate for all occasions. You cannot go wrong if you follow my cautious, conservative, middle-of-the-road approach to your appearance. And never forget what you were told in school: "Neatness Counts."

Julie Hughes and Barry Moss sum it up succinctly when they advise performers to look "absolutely appropriate and great!"

7. YOUR CREDITS AND EXPERIENCE

This is based, of course, on what appears on your résumé. People are more than willing to hire fresh talent, so an extensive list of credits is not de rigueur if you are right for a particular role. (See Appendix B for more specific advice about the look and content of your résumé.)

8. YOUR PERSONALITY

"Personality" is arguably the most important variable. And it brings up the single most valuable piece of advice—given to me by a Broadway Director—I can give you about auditioning:

You must make the Director want to work with you in the first thirty seconds of your audition.

For example, Liliane Montevecchi's role in *Nine* was originally intended for a man, but the lady's personality so dazzled Tommy Tune, the Director-Choreographer, and Maury Yeston, the Composer/Lyricist, that after her audition they reconceived the part. Mr. Yeston then wrote the song "Folies Bergères" specifically for her and she went on to win a Tony Award. Similarly, Ben Vereen's Tony Award-winning part in *Pippin* was originally intended for a much older man.

The lesson to be drawn from this is that if you display a knock-out package consisting of charm, a sense of humor, a measure of security, and a great heaping of talent, the people sitting behind the desk in that audition room are going to notice you. And even if there is no place for you in that particular show, you will be remembered for future projects.

Barry Moss says: "Confidence is everything. We love to see people come in who are glad to be there. Performing should be a joyous experience, not a frightening one. Presumably you're in the business because you love to perform. Think of an audition as a small performance that could well lead to a larger and longer one."

9. OR NONE OF THE ABOVE

To confuse matters completely, sometimes getting cast has very little to do with any of the above, as exemplified in this amusing story:

The late James Kirkwood, the Pulitzer Prize-winning coauthor of *A Chorus Line*, began his career as an actor and nightclub performer. During his stint on the then popular television soap *Valiant Lady*, he was informed that he was to audition for the great Tallulah Bankhead, who was set to star in *Welcome, Darlings*, a summer stock package being created and tailored for her. This show was to include some of the material from Ms. Bankhead's disastrous edition of the *Ziegfeld Follies*, which closed during its pre-Broadway tryout a few months prior. Mr. Kirkwood was to meet her at her town house because she did not want to go to the theatre.

He was extremely nervous when he arrived at her home in the East Sixties in Manhattan. She was still getting dressed upstairs, and he could hear her yelling at one of her dogs, "Delores, stop that! Get out of there, Delores!"

Finally, she came down the stairs, picking at her eyelashes. "Hello, darling. I just got up and I always get this garbage in my eyes when I wake up. Do you have all that crap in your eyes when you wake up?" Nonplussed, he answered, "Yes, of course I do."

Peering at him, she said, "James Kirkwood, right? I've seen you on the soap opera. I like you very much; I like your acting. Somebody told me you were a nightclub comic too. What kind of material do you do? Do you have anything you can audition for me now?"

"Actually," he said, dreading the idea of doing his nightclub-styled satire for an audience of one in a living room in the middle of the afternoon, "I have a takeoff on the *Reader's Digest*—"

Tallulah interrupted, "When I was in the *Follies*, I had a number and I came down the stairs…" She proceeded to sing and act out the entire song.

"Now darling, tell me, what kind of comedy do you do? I don't want a vulgar comedian like David Burns. I want somebody young and clean and you look right, but I have to know what kind of stuff you do."

Once again, he tried, "Well, I have this takeoff on the *Reader's Digest*—"

"When I was in London," Tallulah interrupted, and launched into another lengthy story.

The rest of the afternoon was the same: Mr. Kirkwood never got to do his prepared piece, he just listened to Tallulah.

At last, she sat down next to him on the sofa and said, "Well, darling, I just think you're perfect. You're funny, you're witty, I love what you do, and you look right. I'm going to have an entirely young cast, and I think you've got the part."

Suddenly she swung her legs up onto his lap, pulled the bottoms of her pants up, and said, "Have you ever seen more beautiful ankles than these, darling?"

Getting Your Foot in the Door

Auditioning for Broadway has become an "Event" which one can do only a very few times a year rather than something which one can do a dozen or more times a year. Because work is so scarce, the people with medium talent aren't getting near the Broadway scene because the people with great talent are all available. So the level of professionalism at Broadway auditions is astoundingly high. Any newcomer has to match that level of professionalism or be bypassed. But don't think that newcomers don't have a chance. That is absolutely not true. All Directors and Writers are excited by the possibility of discovering fresh talent at an audition. There is a certain kind of thrill that comes when an actor or actress unknown to the production team displays the talent and the vitality necessary for the show. If you demonstrate that you have the talent, the guts and the confidence to hold your own in the Broadway arena, you will eventually get your chance.

Actor's Equity has certain strictly mandated rules regarding auditions for Broadway productions. For example, every musical running on Broadway which employs a chorus must hold open calls for Eligible Performers every six months, whether or not there are openings in the cast! (Please contact Actors' Equity Association, 165 West 46 Street, New York, NY 10036 for requirements for Eligibility.) If you are deemed "Ineligible" (by virtue of not being employed a certain number of weeks by a theatre maintaining "professional standards"— again, Actors' Equity will give you full information about this upon request) there still is a provision by which you could possibly be seen, after all Equity members and Equity Eligible performers have had their turns. By being persistent and attending enough of these mandatory auditions—or any open call, for that matter—you will eventually be seen and get your chance to show your stuff.

HOW TO ARRANGE AN AUDITION

If you want to get into a show currently running on Broadway, drop your picture and résumé off at the stage door. The doorman will give it to the Stage Manager and he in turn will send it over to the Casting Director. The Casting Directors are very interested in knowing who the new people in town are—people who have not auditioned before for this casting team—because most likely the existing talent pool has already been seen for this particular production. This is especially true in the case of shows which have been running for a long time.

The more sophisticated version of the above paragraph is to know what a specific running show needs, in terms of talent. If you are particularly strong in one certain area, say, tapping, you would target a show like *Crazy for You* (which needs a chorus who can tap dance). Do your homework. See the show, if you can afford it. If not, at least get the playbill and look at the credits. Find out who the Casting Director is, then drop a picture and résumé off at the casting office with a brief note, telling about your experience, even if it just consists of high school productions. The doors to some casting offices are locked—you can't just walk in—but you can always slip your picture (and the note) under the door.

Auditions for any production are arranged in three ways: by public announcement, through an agent, or through a Casting Director.

PUBLIC ANNOUNCEMENTS

When you are starting out you will have to rely on public announcements to learn of open auditions. It is vitally important to be in contact with other actors either through a classroom or a social situation. Wherever actors gather there is sure to be a bulletin board where productions that are holding open auditions will put up some sort of notification.

In the professional theatre world, two weekly trade publications which appear on the newsstands every Thursday serve as public bulletin boards. Originating in New York, *Backstage* covers the East Coast theatrical scene. And in Los Angeles, *Dramalogue* covers the West Coast.

Read thoroughly the publication which originates nearest where you live, for it contains not only casting notices, but a wealth of useful information. Another weekly (national) publication, *Variety*, at one time also had casting notices, but alas, no more. This does not diminish its value to you as a performer. *Variety* is still considered a "must-read" for the entertainment industry.

What follows are some actual casting announcements culled from recent editions of *Backstage:*

"WEST SIDE STORY," U.S. & JAPAN

3/29, 3/30, & 3/31 from 9:30AM -5:30PM at the AEA Audition Center, 165 W. 46 St., 2nd fl., NYC.

Casting for the international Equity Bus & Truck Tour of "West Side Story." Barry Brown, et al., prod'rs; Alan Johnson (reproducing Jerome Robbins' original staging), dir.-choreo. Rehearsals in New York begin July 31. Opens in Detroit in early September, then tours U.S. and Japan. Note: All of the teenagers should look 17-18, but be of legal age to travel without a guardian or parent. Some of the parts listed as Jets and Sharks are chorus (pink) contracts. Chorus auditions will be held on a future date. Sides for Doc, Shank, Krupke, and Gladhand; all others should sing standard Broadway—from the show is fine. Auditions are at the AEA Audition Center, 165 W. 46 St., 2nd fl., NYC. EQ. B&T CONTRACT.

Wed. March 29—Eligible performers, 9:30AM - 5:30 PM.

Thurs. March 30—Eligible performers, 9:30 AM-5:30PM.

Fri. March 31—Eligible performers, 9:30AM - 5:30PM.

Seeking—**Tony:** All-American teenager, great high baritone, good actor; **Maria:** Puerto Rican teenager, great soprano, beautiful, sweet look; **Anita:** early 20's, Maria's cousin, great dancer, strong high belt voice; **Doc:** 50-60, runs the local hangout/ candy store, sweet and good-natured, does not sing; **Lt. Shrank:** late 30's-late 40's, tough and menacing local cop, hates his job, does not sing; **Krupke:** mid 30's to mid 40's, Shrank's assistant, big, dumb cop, does not sing; **Gladhand:** 40's, ineffective high school teacher, does not sing; **The Jets:** Caucasian gang of teenagers, great dancers and strong singers, includes Riff, Action, A-rab, Baby John, Snowboy, Mouthpiece, Big Deal; **Anybody's:** a teenage (female) tomboy who hangs out with the Jets, great dancer and good singer; **The Sharks:** the Puerto Rican gang of teenagers, great dancers, strong singers, include Bernardo, Chino, and others.

MINORITIES, "PHANTOM...OPERA"

3/24 from 10AM - 5:30PM at the AEA Audition Center, 165 W. 46 St., 2nd fl., NYC.

"The Phantom of the Opera," all U.S. companies, will hold an eligible and open audition for minority performers at the AEA Audition Center, 165 W. 46 St., 2nd fl., NYC. Andrew Lloyd Webber, music; Charles Hart, lyrics; Cameron Mackintosh and The Really Useful Theatre Company, prod'rs; Harold Prince, dir.; Gillian Lynne, choreo.; Steve McCorkle, prod. supervisor; David Caddick and Kristin Blodgette, prod. mus'l supervisor; Johnson-Liff Casting Associates, casting dirs. Sing from the standard opera/operetta repertoire, foreign language or English, or legit musical songs which show off range. You may sing from "The Phantom of the Opera," but do not sing "Music of the Night." Do not sing contemporary theatre or pop music under any circumstances. The producer is seeking all minorities who are seriously interested in possible future replacements in all U.S. companies. They are especially looking for African-American, Hispanic, and Asian performers. EQUITY PRODUCTION CONTRACT.

Fri. March 24—Eligible and non-eligible performers, 10AM–5:30 PM (sign-up at 8:30AM).

Seeking—**Christine Daae:** 20s, beautiful young singer, soprano voice that combines elements of classical and pop singing, a light, floaty soprano, sings briefly to high E; **The Phantom:** 30s-40s, high baritone or tenor with a good low range from low A-flat high A-flat, needs a dynamic, bravura, "star" performance, both frightening and irresistible; **Raoul:** late 20s to early 30s, dashing, handsome young aristocrat, high baritone (two octave range form A-flat to A-flat); **Firmin and Andre:** late 30's to 50ish, the managers of the Páris Opera House, trying to be elegant, slightly befuddled and bumbling, need good instincts for stylish comedy, baritones (one sings to A, one to G); **Carlotta Giudicelli:** 30s to 40s, the prima donna of the Paris opera House, a diva in every sense of the word, coloratura soprano (to high E); **Madame Giry:** late 30s to early 50s, the Opera's ballet mistress, an ominous, stern, forbidding figure, mezzo soprano to high B-flat; **Meg Giry:** late teens to early 20s, a member of the Corps de Ballet, must dance on pointe and sing mezzo soprano to G; **Ubaldo Piangi:** late 30s-50s, the opera's leading tenor, Italian-style singer, sings to high C; **Don Attilio/Passarino:** chorus contract, 30s-40s, bass or bass baritone with a solid and legitimate low F, should be a physically interesting character with a good sense of comedy; **Wardrobe Mistress/Confidante:** chorus contract, 30s-40s, contralto or low mezzo, physically interesting character woman, short and round, or tall and thin; and **Monsieur Reyer:** chorus contract, 30s-40s, tenor, character role, the vocal coach of the Paris Opera, an agitated, finicky, meticulous fellow, a strict disciplinarian, always on the verge of hysteria, could be played slightly fey.

These two blurbs contain cast breakdowns for their shows, which were prepared by their Casting Directors. The announcements spell out the principal roles, indicating the ideal types of performers needed. The requirements for these two shows are set in stone; when they say they are looking for a soprano for the role of Maria in *West Side Story*, they mean a soprano. If you belt better than Ethel Merman in her prime, great! But that will never make you a "Maria." When they say that the role of Meg Giry in *The Phantom of the Opera* requires the performer to sing mezzo soprano as well as dance on pointe you'd better hightail it to ballet class (only if your vocal range is right) if you want to play this part. Do you recall the discussion earlier about knowing your type? Here's where your self-critical eye is needed to be able to tell if anything in the breakdown sounds like a possible role for you.

If a currently running show is seeking replacements—as in the above announcement for *The Phantom of the Opera*—they'll always stay close to the essence of the character (type-wise), even to the point of hiring exact clones of the actors they are now employing.

STARBUCK, "110 IN THE SHADE"

The Oldcastle Theatre Company is currently accepting pictures and résumés for the role of **Starbuck** in the musical "110 in the Shade." Rehearsals begin June 20 for a July production under and Equity SPT contract. Oldcastle is an Equal Opportunity Employer. Send pix & résumés to Oldcastle Theatre Company, PO Box 1555, Bennington, VT 05201. EQ. SPT CONTRACT.

PIRELLI, "SWEENEY TODD"

5/24 from 10AM - 1PM at Musical Theatre Works, 440 Lafayette St., 5th fl., NYC.

The Hanger Theatre in Ithaca, NY is holding an open call for non-Equity actors for the role of **Pirelli** in "Sweeney Todd" (Rachel Lampert, dir.). Rehearsals begin June 6, with performances from June 29 - July 15. Seeking a comic tenor with a high-C. Auditions will be held on Wed. May 24 from 10AM -1PM at Musical Theatre Works, 440 Lafayette St., 5th fl., NYC. Prepare music from show or appropriate music that shows range. Accompanist will be provided. Pay. NON-EQUITY PERFORMERS.

These two notices are for specific roles in their respective shows. Note that unlike the first two casting notices above, these next two don't give much information about the parts or the shows. You are expected to know on your own before coming in to audition. If you are a "Starbuck" or a "Pirelli" type and don't recognize the character names (being unfamiliar with their shows) you would inadvertently pass up these auditions. And what a shame, for they might've led to your big break! (Later on in this book I will go into greater detail the need for being familiar with the repertoire of the musical theatre.)

OKLAHOMA, LYRIC THEATRE

3/29 from 11Am-4PM at the AEA Audition Center, 165 W. 46 St., 2nd fl., NYC.

Eligible performer auditions for the Lyric Theatre's 1995 summer season will be held at the AEA Audition Center, 165 W. 46St., 2nd fl., NYC. Season includes: "Evita," "The Unsinkable Molly Brown," "Camelot," "The Secret Garden," and "She Loves Me." Prepare one brief piece (your best and most appropriate audition material), not to exceed two minutes. You may be asked for another piece. Additional auditions by appointment only. Photos and resumes may be submitted to James Rocco, Producing Director, Lyric Theatre, 2501 N. Blackwelder, Oklahoma City, OK 73106. No phone calls or faxes. EQ. GA CONTRACt.

Wed. March 29—Eligible performers, 11AM-4PM.

This last announcement describes a season of shows at one theatre and, as you can plainly see, there is NO cast breakdown or listing of specific roles. Here, your knowledge of the shows and how you might fit in to them is mandatory, and your manipulation of that knowledge could very well get you cast. Especially if you are right for more than one of the productions. If you choose to audition for a company like this one you should perform a song which would immediately make the casting team see you in a specific role in one of these shows. You wouldn't necessarily perform something from one of these shows, but something which evokes the spirit of the part(s) you have in mind for yourself.

If the audition notice is for a new show, it may be worth your while to attempt to be seen even if you do not immediately visualize yourself in one of the parts described in the cast breakdown. There's still a little leeway because, as I mentioned earlier, the show can change if the creative team gets excited about a particular performer.

Whenever you respond to any public announcement, you must follow the preprinted instructions to the letter. Because of the sheer numbers of people who will show up for any casting call posted in the newspaper, the odds will tip ever so slightly in your favor if you read it carefully and don't vary from the directives. You do remember the reason lots of people fail tests, don't you? It's because they don't follow the instructions. Don't fail the "audition test!"

AGENTS

In the first round of casting, someone designated by the production company (usually the Casting Director) prepares and sends a casting breakdown (like those in the ads above) to all reputable agents. Each agent will then go through his client list and send ("submit") photos and résumés of potential choices for each role. The agent should propose not only obvious choices from his roster, but also available performers who would be more off-beat options. The Casting Director will then go through those submissions, selecting some (but not all!) to be auditioned. Most shows will cast most of the major roles through this process.

So how do you get an agent? Not that easy. There's a bit of a "Catch-22" involved in that an agent usually won't want to take you on as a client unless he thinks he can do something for you, and he won't usually be able to do much if you don't have some solid credits behind you. But an agent can do a lot if he believes in you and your talent.

If you are agent-less, try to attend as many auditions as you can, just to get work. Anywhere. Build your credits. In New York, either the agent himself or a representative from his office sees the important projects, with an eye towards looking out for new talent to represent. Work begets work.

If you do have an agent and you are not being sent out often, or often enough, or (heaven forbid!) not at all, you must change agents. An agent works for you. Repeat this until you can recite it by rote.

CASTING DIRECTORS

The Casting Director is the modern version of the 1930's Talent Scout. A Casting Director is hired to present the choices from which the production's stage Director selects the cast for the show. I spoke with two of New York's top Casting Directors, Julie Hughes and Barry Moss. Partners for many years, their office casts projects in all media: theatre, film, television and recordings.

JULIE HUGHES: "We read a script, then we send a breakdown to the agents in town, who send back submissions from their pool of clients. We don't cast only from their submissions; going through them triggers other ideas, other performers."

BARRY MOSS: "If there was no Casting Director, the show's stage Director would have to wade through thousands of people who are not right for the project; we save the Director an enormous amount of time."

JULIE HUGHES: "We also try to make a creative contribution to the show by coming up with concepts which are totally alien to anything that has been suggested before, but which we think might work. This includes non-traditional casting."

Casting Directors need to be very familiar with the available talent pool.

JULIE HUGHES: "We try to see as many workshops and musical presentations as we can. Also, since we have multiple projects going on, we are auditioning all the time. If a performer comes in for one project and isn't right for it, he may be absolutely wonderful for another handled by our office."

BARRY MOSS: "Actors are the tools of our work. We want to be exposed to as many actors as possible, so our doors are open. We train our receptionist to know everything that our office is doing, so the receptionist will notify us if someone walks in whom he thinks may be right for one of our projects."

JULIE HUGHES: "The receptionist brings the picture back to me and I ask, 'Is this girl as pretty as her picture?' and he will tell me, 'Yes, and I think she'd be right for the ingenue in the new play we're doing.' So Barry or I will come out and meet her and possibly set her up for an audition.

What qualities make a performer castable?

BARRY MOSS: "Confidence. If people don't believe in themselves, why should anyone else believe in them?"
JULIE HUGHES: "And we do believe in everyone we bring in to audition for a show. We want them to get the jobs."

Unfair as it may seem, often the only way you can get an audition scheduled for a principal role in a major Broadway production is through the Agent–Casting Director route. That's merely a fact of life, in the You-Can't-Fight-City-Hall Department. If you don't have an agent now, you will get one in time. If you are not presently known by a casting office, I have given you ideas on how you can be. In the meantime, there are plenty of auditions listed in the trade papers that you can attend right now.

Preparation Part I

SELECTING MATERIAL

Where to Find an Accompanist

If you are starting from ground zero, the first thing to do is to link up with a pianist who will help you find, prepare, and rehearse your material.

So where do you find an accompanist? Easy.

Anywhere.

Anyone who plays the piano is a potential accompanist. Yes, there is an art to accompanying; but for now, anyone will do—a friend, neighbor, voice teacher, or a relative are all good people to begin with. If they can't or won't play for you, ask if they know someone—you will undoubtedly find someone to work with through a recommendation.

Accompanists advertise in the trade papers and also post their business cards up on the bulletin boards at rehearsal studios. Pick a few at random, call them up, and talk over the phone. Ask the price and where the sessions are held—in their home or in a studio. Find one who gives you good vibes on the phone and arrange a session. No one can promise that the first time will work out for everyone, so if you don't like the person, find another quickly via the same means. At least now you'll have some basis for comparison.

As your credits grow and you get more accomplished, you will meet new people and thus be exposed to new musicians. Eventually, you'll be able to recognize the difference between good and bad pianists, and you will establish a rapport with certain musicians with whom you prefer to work.

But for starters, find anyone who seems suitable, and begin.

Your Audition Repertoire

You have to have something to do at an audition to demonstrate your talent. At an audition for a play you read, for a musical you sing. You can't just sing anything. From the vast repertoire of material to choose from, you will have to carefully select a group of songs which will exhibit your talent in such a way as to make others want to use you in their productions. Any song you sing will immediately establish the quality of your vocal instrument. But a really cleverly chosen audition song will illuminate your soul. And if the casting team gets a glimpse of something inside you, something behind your eyes, the odds are better that they will be intrigued enough to want to hire you.

Thus, you must not hurry this part of your preparation.

The first criteria for selecting audition songs is to find material with which you connect emotionally and which complements your age and appearance.

EMOTIONAL CONSIDERATIONS Although your first choice for any song should of course be one you can sing believably without too much strain, you do not have to "agree" with all the lyrics of a song. If you have chosen an interesting song but the lyrics don't espouse your personal beliefs, you can still use it. Be someone else for those few minutes. Create a character to sing the song. Act.

CHRONOLOGICAL CONSIDERATIONS Anyone under the age of about forty should not sing, "Send In The Clowns" from *A Little Night Music* or "I'm Still Here" from *Follies* or "Before The Parade

Passes By" from *Hello, Dolly!*. It is disorienting to see someone young, with no obvious backlog of experience, sing songs whose words were written to reflect the experiences of a more mature person. The reverse is also true with songs like "I Feel Pretty" from *West Side Story* and "Tomorrow" from *Annie*. These sound better coming from a younger person.

At the end of the day (as they say in London), just understand that the song must suit you. Lyricist Sheldon Harnick (*Fiorello!, She Loves Me, Fiddler on the Roof*) remembers an audition for one of his shows at which the Stage Manager came out and announced the next performer, someone with an African name. Out walked a tall, majestic-looking young black man carrying a Conga drum. He was wearing what appeared to be colorful African ceremonial robes, which made him look like a tribal chief. He strode to center stage, put the drum in front of him, and struck it several times with the palm of his hand. Mr. Harnick and his cohorts were primed for some wild, stirring, primitive chant. Instead, in a high nasal tenor, the actor launched into "On The Street Where You Live," a capella, except for an occasional blow to the drum. The effect was so ludicrously incongruous that those watching the audition could only laugh—it was impossible for them to evaluate the performer's talent. P.S. The man wasn't trying to be funny!

As you search for the songs to fit your portfolio, you will discard many songs because they aren't right. You will probably be disappointed and frustrated. But if you are diligent you will find there are dozens of candidates to choose from that will fit your age, range, and personality. Don't fret about not singing the ones you like that don't.

BUILDING A SONG PORTFOLIO

Everyone is at the very least expected to have prepared two songs: a "ballad" and an "up-tune."

At its simplest, a ballad should show your emotional range and the way you phrase a lyric—your sensitivity to the words and thoughts.

An up-tune should show your sense of rhythm and how exciting you are as a performer. As a by-product, it can imply how enjoyable you would be in the cast. There are always so many problems attached to putting on a show that no one wants to work with people perceived as boring or unpleasant. So find a zingy up-number that shows off your sense of humor and sense of fun. Try to dazzle them. There is no rule anywhere that says you can't entertain at an audition. If you are able to unselfconsciously divert the people casting a show, you may find yourself in the cast as a result.

The best kind of audition number in either category is a humorous one. The worst kind of number in either category is a song of self-pity. The latter type makes the listener uncomfortable, whereas the former allows the listener to sit back and relax. In tandem, the ballad and the up-tune provide a needed contrast for the listeners. And the two should be as different as possible in order to show the greatest contrast.

Okay, ready for this one? I know that just two songs aren't enough. You must prepare more than two. If you spark interest from the Director or one of the Writers, they may need to see you show values other than the ones demonstrated in your ballad or up-tune, so it is advisable to prepare several different types of songs and to have them in performance-shape at all times. You should build a song portfolio—a whole collection of songs you will use as your audition pieces. In this portfolio you should have at least one of each of the following types of songs:

1. Ballad
2. Up-tune
3. Comedy song
4. "Contemporary Broadway" song
5. Patter song
6. Standard torch song (only for women)

and if this style of music suits you, you might also add:

7. Rock 'n Roll song

At almost every audition I have ever played, someone sitting behind the decision-table has asked to hear a song from these categories. Too many times performers have only two songs prepared—sometimes only one—and when asked for additional material, instead of saying, "No, I haven't prepared anything else," they try to improvise something with the pianist. Instead of impressing the production team with their versatility, they generally make a mess of their audition. It's better to have more material prepared than you think you will use.

COMEDY SONGS

The very notion of having to sing a comedy song throws performers and coaches alike into such a tizzy—as if they had never even heard of the concept before. This is probably because good comedy songs are notoriously difficult to find. The same songs tend to be used over and over. The works of Noel Coward, Howard Dietz, E.Y. Harburg, Lorenz Hart, and Cole Porter—to mention just a few of the immortals—are chock full of great, little-known, sure-fire comic material. Finding these songs takes a lot of digging, but they are there to be found.

Always keep in mind that the people auditioning you are usually frighteningly well-versed in the standard musical theatre song repertoire. This means that it will be a virtually impossible task to find a comedy song that your judges can't recite along with you. Do not let this fact intimidate you—just do not expect laughs where laughs should be, and do not under any circumstances attempt to perform all the extant verses of the song you select. Just once through the main melody will be sufficient to demonstrate your way with comic material.

The best kind of comedy songs are ones in which the character has a huge problem and is trying to explain it. For the character, the situation is serious. For the listener, it's hilarious. For example, in "I Cain't Say No," from *Oklahoma!*, Ado Annie is in a "turrible fix." The more upset she is about her situation, the funnier it is for the listener. If the actress performs the song "cutesy," trying to "tell jokes" instead of just be in character, it will not be even the slightest bit humorous for the listener.

At one audition, all the actors were asked to prepare a comedy song. A young man entered the room and said, "I don't have a comedy song so I'll just sing 'Being Alive' very fast and see if it's funny." It wasn't.

Here's a terribly dangerous idea (NOTE: Only try this if you are desperate for material): Take a standard song that everyone knows and is sick of and rewrite the lyrics a la Allan Sherman's classic parodies. Be careful—your rewrite must be very clever and you must never do it in front of the original writers.

CONTEMPORARY BROADWAY SONGS

If you are auditioning for one of the new "pop-operas," like any of the shows with music by Andrew Lloyd Webber, Claude-Michel Schönberg, or Frank Wildhorn, the standard Broadway repertoire won't do. You should have songs from these types of shows under your belt.

PATTER SONGS

A "patter song" is one that has a complicated, wordy lyric which often serves as a showcase tour-de-force for the lyricist. The melody in patter songs takes a subservient role to the lyric. Every Gilbert and Sullivan operetta has at least one—and any of them will suffice. Cole Porter, Noel Coward, and Lorenz Hart each wrote many of them. Another recent example is "Another Hundred People" from *Company*—although, as I will discuss later, you would be wise to avoid Stephen Sondheim's songs.

TORCH SONGS

Prime examples would be "The Man That Got Away," from the movie *A Star Is Born*, by Harold Arlen and Ira Gershwin; "The Man I Love," by the Gershwin Brothers—George and Ira—; and "Bill," from *Show Boat*, by Jerome Kern, P.G. Wodehouse, and Oscar Hammerstein II. Linda Ronstadt recorded 32 suitable torch/ballads for her albums "What's New" and "Lush Life," and "For Sentimental

Reasons." Check your Judy Garland and Barbra Streisand records for some choice, little-known ones.

ROCK 'N' ROLL SONGS

Please pick one with a pretty, singable melody. Although the theme song from the motion picture *Shaft* may have won the Academy Award as best song of its year, it hardly has a catchy lyric. Turn instead to something soft-rock, such as songs by Neil Diamond, Dan Fogelberg, Billy Joel, Melissa Manchester, Randy Newman, Paul Simon, Jimmy Webb, or Stevie Wonder. (Later on in this book, you will find more detailed information about auditioning for rock shows.)

You may want to add a Country-Western song to the above list. Although it is rarely called for, it couldn't hurt to have one ready.

Steel yourself—here's another zinger:
You should also have a back-up song ready for each of the categories. Why?
Because what if the person just ahead of you—and this happens all the time!—sings the same song you were planning to do. Now don't say, "But that happened to me and I know I sang the song a hundred times better than the one who did it before me." That may indeed be true, but please understand the view of the people listening. They don't want to be bored by hearing the identical song twice in a row. That's why you have—and should use—your back-up song.

I once played the auditions for the touring company of *The Wiz*. Eighteen people in a row—I counted—sang either "God Bless The Child" or "Be A Lion," and not one person brought another song to even offer a choice. It drove the Director and the Choreographer mad because after a short while the actors lost their individuality; it was difficult afterwards to remember accurately who sang better than who.

If you have talent, your alternate choice will show it off just as well as your first choice. After all, didn't you choose both on the basis of their ability to do just that?

Select a song because you love it; because you think it's great; because you can perform the hell out of it. Don't pick any song just because you heard someone else do it; because you don't really like it but you think others will; or because you don't have a better one.

In speaking with many colleagues while preparing this book, certain bits of advice cropped up fairly consistently. Casting Director Barry Moss is not alone when he offers this guidance: "One of the most common mistakes people make is to think they have to show their entire range—from their lowest note to their highest note—at a single audition. You should choose a song that fits most comfortably in your range. If the Musical Director wants something different he'll ask for it. Meanwhile you've put your best foot forward and that increases your confidence."

So don't rule out songs just because you can do *more* than the song allows you to.

People are always uncertain about how long their songs should be. The quick answer: No more than two minutes for each song. The people auditioning you make an immediate judgment based on your look as soon as you enter the room. They are also extremely practiced listeners and can tell rather quickly whether or not you have the requisite vocal ability; some Musical Directors boast that they know within the first eight bars of a song. So doing a long song with many choruses is rather an imposition, no matter how good you are. You can make a clear case for your talent in a very short time. If your song goes on for too long, there is a great possibility that you will be cut off midstream. I promise you, you won't be a happy camper if this happens.

Boy, my advice unnerves you, doesn't it? You think that you need at least a few minutes to develop a character, don't you? No, you don't. Remember the expression "leave them wanting more?" If you doubt the wisdom of this, take a look at the W.C. Fields movie *The Old Fashioned Way*. In it, Fields is forced to hear Cleopatra Pepperday—an untalented, wealthy woman—audition for him. He wants her money to put on a creaky melodrama in her town. She wants to be in the show, so in her living room he listens to her sing "The

Seashell Song." At the end of the first chorus, Fields politely rises from his seat, applauds, and starts to heartily and insincerely congratulate her as if it were the end of the song, only to have her launch into the next verse. This continues a few more times. Mr. Fields' hilarious facial expressions and antics are representative of what the casting team goes through when you sing long songs.

Use two minutes as the maximum time for your audition song. If your favorite song takes considerably longer than that to make a complete statement lyrically, choose another song.

What Not to Sing

I freely admit that the opinions in this section are the most debatable and subjective written herein, but they do come from experience (mine and others). Sometimes I feel that singers resist my advice merely because it means they have to do some homework—once I have eliminated 99 percent of the songs they know as potential audition material, they are left with some hard work in front of them, finding and selecting what are considered to be better choices.

Certain kinds of songs don't do the wonders for you you think they will if you sing them. They can be grouped into the following categories:

ANYTHING EXTREMELY WELL-KNOWN

As I mentioned before, more often than not the people auditioning you can sing along with any of the familiar songs from Broadway shows, even from the unsuccessful ones. They like those songs. They may even love some of those songs. But hearing them in an audition situation is, frankly, boring. The purpose of an audition is to make the Director pay close attention to you and give you serious consideration. Well, one way to accomplish this from your point of view is to sing something the Director doesn't know by heart.

One woman protested, "But I thought people like to hear familiar songs?" Yes, they do, but not at an audition. You must perk them up—in a sense, force them to listen closely. You cannot accomplish that if you lull them with the familiarity of your material.

So at the center of my arguments about auditions is the theory that you should sing well-crafted material which is not well-known; actually, the more obscure the better.

However, there seems to be an exception to this. When I played auditions for a Country-Western show, the listeners greatly appreciated it when someone came in with a Country-Western standard rather than an obscure song in the genre. The difference in quality between the Nashville hits and the misses is significant, so if you are auditioning for that kind of show and you can't find a dynamite unknown song, don't look too hard. Stick with a well-known one that has a great, singable melody and actable lyrics.

OVERDONE SONGS

Performers almost never get together and compare their audition material with an eye toward exclusivity, so it is an unfortunate fact that any song could be part of more than one person's repertoire. You cannot avoid this. But you can, and indeed you must, diminish the possibility of singing a song which lots of other people choose. Overdone songs have virtually no impact on the listener and are much more of a hindrance to you than are the "well-known" songs discussed above.

If I had $1.00 for every woman who auditions with Irving Berlin's "I Love a Piano" I'd be not rich, but able to take a wonderful vacation. Not only overdone, it is also almost always performed in an identical manner. Illustrating their adoration for the instrument, most of the singers rub against, fondle, or climb all over the piano in the room, sometimes inadvertently knocking the sheet music to the floor in their fervor. Frequently they even turn their attention to the accompanist, as if the lyric were "I Love a Pianist." As amusing as the lyric is, this song is not a comedy song, despite its being performed when a comedy song is requested. I suggest it be permanently retired from people's audition repertoire.

Overdone songs are certainly not a new phenomenon. A scene in the 1958 Broadway musical, *Say, Darling* (a "backstage" story about the creation of a Broadway musical) satirically depicted an audition for singers. All you have to know to enjoy this scene is that the smash hit, *My Fair Lady*, opened a mere two years prior and its songs were still in the process of taking the world by storm.

> The first woman, a soprano, enters and sings "I Could Have Danced All Night." After two lines, the producer stops her with a polite "Thank you." The lady exits. A second woman, an alto, enters and gives her music to the pianist. She too sings "I Could Have Danced All Night" and is stopped even quicker than her predecessor. The third auditioner, a man, enters and sings "Old Man River." The producer stops him in the middle of the second line. Finally the fourth audition-er, a woman (an alto) enters and announces that she will sing a piece of special material; distinguishing herself from the others even further, she has brought along her own accompa-nist. She belts the verse to her song, a dramatic, passionate, over-ripe torch-song. Then she reaches the chorus, which turns out to be nothing less than "I Could Have Danced All Night." This time all the listeners present (not just the pro-ducer) stop her immediately.

To help in your selections, I have listed in Appendix A the names of songs that are considered the most overdone at auditions. Avoid anything on this list, which was compiled in the years preceding this writing, 1995. Obviously, as tastes and times change, so will the list. When in doubt, ask questions—and listen to the answers!

If you find that you are using any song on the list, I really feel that you should replace it with a viable substitute post haste. Oh, I can hear you now, protesting, "But I use that song and I always get jobs with it." Well then, in your case I'm truly happy to be proved wrong—but you are an anomaly.

"SIGNATURE" SONGS–THOSE CLOSELY ASSOCIATED
WITH A PARTICULAR SINGER

If, for example, you sing "Over The Rainbow," the listeners will unconsciously and involuntarily compare you with Judy Garland. No matter how good you are, when you sing something closely associated with another singer you can't make people forget the original rendition. You want *your* talent evaluated and, hopefully, appreciated. You don't want your valuable audition time spent standing in someone else's shadow.

I'll never forget the young man who sang the Barbra Streisand slowed-down arrangement of "Happy Days Are Here Again," complete with Streisand-like arm gestures. He was genuinely surprised and a little miffed when, after he sang, the Director suggested the man sing something on his own and not flagrantly copy someone else's style.

At one audition a few years ago, a young lady sang "Nothing" from *A Chorus Line*. After the song, the Director took her aside and explained that because she did a song that was from a show (then) currently running on Broadway, it was difficult to evaluate her particular gifts. He went on to say that the song wasn't an especially good choice because the exquisite performance by the original actress, Priscilla Lopez, was so ingrained in the memories of everyone looking at this girl that they couldn't get a clear sense of what she could really do. He advised her to prepare another song and come to the callback. Tears began to well up in her eyes. She said, "My mother told me I do this song better than Priscilla Lopez."

ONE-JOKE SONGS

High on the list of songs to avoid are humorous songs with only one joke, or songs with a single "gimmick." Once the listener knows the joke or is in on the gimmick, the element of surprise has been taken away and the song is usually pretty dull on repeated hearings. It would take the comedic skills of a Robin Williams or a Joan Rivers to make a joke we have heard before sound fresh. Songs in this category include:

"Make It Another Old Fashioned, Please"—*Panama Hattie*

TOO CHEERFUL

Try to put yourself in your listener's place when you select your material. Remember that, depending on the time of your audition, they either have a long day ahead of or behind them. Taking this into consideration, stay away from songs that are spiritually or morally uplifting—"You'll Never Walk Alone" *(Carousel)*; relentlessly cheerful—"On A Wonderful Day Like Today" *(The Roar of the Greasepaint...)*; or so cloyingly sweet as to send the listeners instantly into a diabetic coma (too many examples to mention, and you already know who wrote them). Tommy Tune has said that he prefers songs with a positive outlook. Perfect. Don't take this to the extreme.

TOO DEPRESSING

Don't bring your listeners down with songs illuminating a pessimistic view of the world, of love, etc. Examples:

"Spring Can Really Hang You Up The Most"
"(Have I Stayed) Too Long At The Fair"—*The Billy Barnes Revue*
"This Funny World"—*Betsy*
"Everybody Loves You When You're Asleep"—*I'd Rather Be Right*

TOO BOASTFUL

I'll let you in on a secret. Ssh! Don't tell anyone that I'm a stool-pigeon, but songs of self-aggrandizement provoke perverse thoughts in the listener. Examples:

"I'm The Greatest Star" *According to whom?*
"You're Gonna Hear From Me" *Not if I have anything to say about it!*
"I've Gotta Be Me" *But why?*
"Nothing Can Stop Me Now" *Oh, yeah? I can!*

TOO SELF-DEPRECATING

Although they work brilliantly in their original theatrical contexts, songs which portray the singer in a negative light do just that for you when you are auditioning. So don't sing songs which make you out as a loser. Examples:

"Nobody Does It Like Me"—*Seesaw*
"But Not For Me"—*Girl Crazy*
"You Can Always Count On Me"—*City of Angels*
"Mr. Cellophane"—*Chicago*

SONGS INTENDED FOR THE OPPOSITE GENDER

In the pop world, a singer doing a song intended for the opposite gender is perfectly acceptable. Songwriters tried hard to make their songs singable by both men and women, even going so far as to write additional lyrics to adjust anything gender-specific. (Ira Gershwin, author of the lyrics to "The Man I Love" wrote an alternate version called "The Girl I Love.") However, at a theatrical audition, you should avoid singing anything not originally intended to be sung by your sex. (Unless it is for comic effect. I will discuss this later on in the book.) A man, auditioning for a production of *The Phantom of the Opera* announced that he would be singing the leading lady's first song "Think Of Me." The conductor sternly called out "No, you're not!" and the man sang something else more appropriate.

ORIGINAL MATERIAL

It's usually not a great idea to sing original songs—either written by yourself, by your pianist, or by your friends—at auditions. These songs are not always as good as you think they are. Being fair about this, obscure show songs are often obscure for very good reasons as well. But if you've made a poor choice, and the song you're perform-ing makes the casting team wish they had brought in earplugs, and someone in the room asks, "Where did you find that song," you're much better off being able to say, "It was cut from *Breakfast at Tiffany's*," rather than saying it was written by a friend. There are exceptions to this, of course, just as there are exceptions to all the points in this book. But bear in mind that Directors have rejected many a performer because of a bad song choice. Why risk it?

SONGS WHICH ARE TOO DIFFICULT

Don't kill yourself at an audition. I feel like I'm divulging a well-kept secret when I tell you it's not necessary to perform a difficult or tricky song to be noticed. That type of number usually contains many pitfalls and traps that you could easily fall into if you are edgy. For a time, the song "What Are You Doing The Rest Of Your Life?" was a popular audition number. It's a stunning song, but it has a melodic line composed of small, chromatic intervals that are hard to sing accurately in the best of circumstances. Over the years many good singers have inadvertently gone off-pitch singing that song. The moral is: Sing something simple. Sing a song that won't work against you if you're nervous.

SONGS WRITTEN BY ANYONE ON THE PRODUCTION TEAM

Unless it is specifically requested in advance, do not sing songs written by the Composer or Authors for whom you are auditioning. The same goes for songs from shows with which the Director, Choreographer, or Musical Director were closely associated. This point was strongly echoed by everyone I spoke to while preparing this book. You are correct if you think they will be flattered by your choice of their material, but since most—if not all—Composers and Lyricists have very definite ideas about how their songs should be performed, they will be busy comparing during your audition, rather than watching and listening.

If you think they will be impressed with your "different," "novel," or "definitive" rendition of their material, you may again be correct—but not under these circumstances. You are there to show off yourself and your talent to best advantage. You don't want to misuse your precious few minutes of audition time distracting your listeners. If they are for any reason whatsoever displeased with your performance of their material, you will have wasted all your preparation and may as well kiss that job good-bye.

You'd be shocked at how many people sing Stephen Sondheim's songs in front of him at auditions. And how many of those people forget (or worse, sing the wrong) lyrics! Mr. Sondheim has been known to correct the culpable on the spot ...

At an audition (in America) for a European production of *Hello, Dolly!* a woman, upon being introduced to the score's composer/lyricist, Jerry Herman, gushed: "I'm so thrilled to meet you, and I'm doubly glad because I picked one of your songs to sing today." Then she sang a song composed by Richard Rodgers.

WHEN TO IGNORE MY ADVICE

You may go against any of the abovementioned advice only when specifically requested by the people auditioning you. For example, when you audition as a replacement in a production that is running or for a touring company of an established show you are often asked to prepare a song from the show and sing that as your audition piece. Taking this request a step further, the *Les Misérables* production staff asked everyone auditioning for the Los Angeles and Canadian production to not only prepare a specific song from the score but to imitate the performance on the cast album as closely as possible. When the production staff wants you to do this they will make their wishes known through the Casting Director. If you do not get a specific request, do not sing songs from the show.

A WORD ON SONDHEIM...

Stephen Sondheim, one of the theatre's few true geniuses, has written the music and lyrics for many brilliant, melodic, witty, singable, and highly actable songs. His material is challenging, complex, and rewarding to perform—not only because he understands the capabilities and limitations of voices, but also because he has a thorough knowledge of the theatre and the possibilities for songs within the framework of a show. Mr. Sondheim conceives his songs as complete one-act plays, with a beginning, a middle, and an end. Many of his songs can stand alone, outside the context of the show, and would therefore seem to make very good audition pieces.

Now for the bad news.

Most people think it inadvisable to sing Mr. Sondheim's songs at auditions.

Quite frankly, his songs are so good they can magnify any flaws in your voice or technique. Remember that the purpose of the audition is to present yourself at your best. And if you are nervous, or have had a particularly busy day prior to the audition, or are not thoroughly warmed up, his songs will not serve you well.

Also, the same rule about people who audition you knowing the songs too well applies doubly here. There are so many songs to pick and choose from that will be better for you during an audition situation than any of Mr. Sondheim's—save his splendid material for your club act.

Where to Find Songs

Although I have been tempted, I can't print a list of the songs that I feel would be appropriate for auditions. As you will see, there are so many possibilities that I would be severely limiting you by even listing a hundred or so. What I can do is tell you where you can find good material. It's not that difficult to do—it just takes time. And considerable research. But trust me, the results will pay off a thousand-fold over the years.

Too many performers know embarrassingly little about the musical theatre. I can't think of any other occupation wherein practitioners are not required to have even a minimal knowledge of their field. Can you imagine a doctor, lawyer, architect, or engineer doing his work without thoroughly knowing the history and craft of his chosen profession, and instead operating solely on "feelings," "gut instincts," and "natural abilities"?

In addition, I believe that every aspiring performer should have a basic knowledge of and familiarity with the songs in all the major musicals that have been performed on Broadway. You can call this part of your training, Doing Your Homework.

The minimum list of shows you should know includes the following:

- The five mega-hit shows by Richard Rodgers and Oscar Hammerstein II: *Oklahoma!*, *Carousel*, *South Pacific*, *The King and I*, and *The Sound of Music*;
- Alan Jay Lerner and Frederick Loewe's: *Brigadoon*, *My Fair Lady*, and *Camelot*;

- Jerry Herman's: *Hello, Dolly!, Mame, Mack and Mabel,* and *La Cage aux Folles;*
- Andrew Lloyd Webber's phenomenal successes: *Evita, Cats,* and *The Phantom of the Opera;*
- Stephen Sondheim's: *A Funny Thing Happened on the Way to the Forum, Company, Follies, A Little Night Music,* and *Sweeney Todd;*
- Along with the following: *A Chorus Line, Annie Get Your Gun, Bells Are Ringing, Cabaret, Damn Yankees, Fiddler on the Roof, Finian's Rainbow, Funny Girl, Guys and Dolls, Gypsy, Kismet, Kiss Me Kate, Les Misérables, Man of la Mancha, Me and My Girl, ShowBoat, The Fantasticks, The Music Man, The Pajama Game,* and *West Side Story.*

This is by no means an exhaustive list. But if at the very least you have a familiarity with these shows, you will have a pretty solid grounding in what a good theatre song is, so when you select your songs you will have a strong basis for comparison. As a by-product, you will have a large list of songs not to sing—ever—at an audition.

Why?

Because most of the songs in the above shows are much too well known—go back to "What Not To Sing" for the explanation. But many's the time a Director has said to a singer something like, "Do you have anything similar to 'It Only Takes a Moment' from *Hello, Dolly!'*—and the singer has sheepishly admitted not knowing "It Only Takes a Moment." Knowing these shows gives you not only a background in your chosen field, but also a common vocabulary with your peers.

Also, the roster of musicals performed in summer stock and dinner theaters across the country is largely culled from the above list, augmented by whatever fairly recent shows have just become available. As you saw for yourself in an earlier chapter of this book, when those theaters put out audition notices in the trades they only list the names of the shows they are doing, not the full cast breakdowns. If you know the shows, you automatically know which roles are right for you.

Okay, now that you have taken the time to do the above, where do you find those "obscure" songs that I promise will work miracles for you?

The answer is coming in just a moment. I have to give you the explanatory buildup first.

Be aware of this: There have been well over 1,000 musicals performed on and off Broadway since the beginning of this century. Each show contains, on an average, 12 to 14 songs. Doing some simple multiplication in round numbers, we're now in the range of about 12,000 songs. Add to this number several hundred film musicals with about 5 or 6 songs in each movie and our total is now well over 13,500. To this total we can, if we wish, add songs that were written strictly for the pop market—or Tin Pan Alley as it was called in an earlier age—and the numbers skyrocket.

I do hear your immediate protests: "Most of those songs aren't that good, or they're not usable for our purposes. After all, your total includes opening choruses and other discountable material."

Fine, I say. Even though I rounded-off on the low side, throw out three-fourths of them and we still have a staggering number to select from.

So, if there are so many to choose from, why do most people pick the same few over and over? Because, admittedly, many—if not most—of the songs I am alluding to are out-of-print, unpublished, or similarly unavailable for easy perusal. So what's left? The readily available standard repertoire. Too easy. You will find your audition material from the following sources:

STAGE PRODUCTIONS

We happen to be living in a lucky era right now. For finding songs, that is. In the last twenty years there have been many revues on (and off) Broadway presenting well-known and not-so-well-known songs by both major and—pardon the easy categorizing—minor theatre composers. Shows such as *Ain't Misbehavin'*, *Eubie!*, *Leader of the Pack*, *1000 Years of Rock and Roll*, *Smokey Joe's Cafe*, *Stardust*, *Sophisticated Ladies*, and *Starting Here, Starting Now*. If you didn't see any of them, perhaps you know someone who was in one who may have the music and could recommend some songs to you. All but two of the above shows were recorded. (The exceptions are *1000 Years of Rock and Roll* and *Stardust*).

RECORDINGS

Ben Bagley's Painted Smiles Record Company issued many albums devoted to the undeservedly lesser-known songs of nearly every famous Broadway songwriter. The records, which contained an average of 15 songs per disc are now out-of-print (as are almost all vinyl records) But the indomitable Mr. Bagley issued them all on compact disc (to date more than 50 are in print). As a boon to disc buyers, most of his CDs have bonus tracks, raising the average to about 20 great songs per disc. Widely available in retail stores—and by mail, directly from the company—they are a treasure trove of great audition material.

Another company, Music Masters, issued over sixty albums containing both previously out-of-print recordings and never-before-issued-on-record material by show and movie composers and lyricists. Their "Music of Broadway" series alone—eighteen discs full of fabulous songs—will provide you with dozens of choices for audition songs. Several of their albums were remastered onto compact discs and are also worth exploring. These will be a bit harder to find, but are worth the effort.

In 1982, a treasure trove of musical theatre materials long presumed "lost" were found in a warehouse in New Jersey. Musical theatre archivists and historians have been busy ever since, exhuming the hundreds of recovered songs (and their original orchestrations) and making this material live again. Because of their scholarship and tenacity, another series of recordings exists which will benefit you, the seeker of rare and obscure material. Particularly noteworthy in this group are the distinguished recordings of Gershwin shows on the Nonesuch label, and all the recordings conducted by John McGlinn on EMI.

A bit harder to find, but well worth the effort to do so, are the compact discs produced by an independent label, Shadowland-Rialto

Recordings. On four of their releases are over 110 songs—most of which would make great audition material.

You should also check out early Frank Sinatra, Dean Martin, Judy Garland and Peggy Lee albums. These singers had great songwriters writing and tailoring material specifically with them in mind, and you just may find a not-too-well-known song to your liking on their recordings, while avoiding the "signature" songs. Obviously there are many more singers to add to the four mentioned—look through and listen to the records in your parents' collection.

So, now you've found a song you like on a recording and you don't have any sheet music. What do you do?

First, you call whichever local store sells sheet music to see if, by chance, they have it—most stores in small neighborhoods have very small selections, though. Check with your musical friends. Look in the piano bench in your parents' home. Call up your piano-playing aunt; if she has the song, she'll be delighted to give it to you. I asked her.

If you've still yielded no results, don't be discouraged. The great search is on! Your next step is to call a store like Colony in New York City, which maintains one of the largest collections—for sale, of course—of in-print sheet music. See if the song is still obtainable. If it isn't available as an individual sheet, the song may be published in one of the hundreds of published collections—including so-called Fake Books—which provide lead vocal lines and chord symbols for about 1,000 songs per book; as well as specialized volumes with generic titles on the order of Great Songs of the 1960s. Several decades worth of these last were issued.

If you have no luck at Colony, or a similar store, call the Music Exchange, also in New York City, which sells its extensive collection of out-of-print music.

If you are still coming a cropper, go to the Library and Museum of the Performing Arts at Lincoln Center. On the first floor, in the music division, there exists a large and unusual collection of out-of-print sheet music, which can be photocopied on the premises for fifteen cents a page. There is an index of songs by title only, so be sure to know the correct title.

The music division of the Library of Congress in Washington D.C. is another resource. They are surprisingly helpful—so long as they are not violating copyright laws.

If you still haven't found the song through any of the aforementioned sources and if the sales help at the stores or the librarians can't recommend anywhere else to try, you can surely get a pianist to write out the music—at least a lead sheet—taking it off the record on which you found it.

Or, have a professional copyist "take-down" or transcribe the song from the record. More on this later.

The above suggestions certainly do not represent the only places to find songs. I offer them merely as a starting point, and I hope my thoughts will inspire and trigger some clever ones of your own. Undoubtedly the pianist with whom you work will have some ideas for you; but please, do not rely on his advice alone without doing some work by yourself.

No, it's not easy, but doing all that listening and research can only help you in the long run. After all, you are immersing yourself in the worlds of theatre and music—could there be more pleasurable homework?

Preparation Part II

THE MECHANICS

How to Prepare Your Music

An astounding number of talented performers who come to auditions appear to be the very model of perfection: smartly dressed, every hair in place, in all visible ways poised and professional. But the music they hand to the pianist is a disaster! Describing their music as distressingly illegible would be too kind.

Also, accompanists often wonder why, with the inexpensive cost and availability of photocopying services, so much music carried to auditions is in large, heavy books. Or why, if an actor's song is not in a book, its pages are usually unattached and in an advanced state of deterioration? Those who *are* aware of their music's condition apologize, saying, "I know I should get another copy of this song." Or they offer an excuse, such as, "I didn't have time to tape the music together."

The only thing I can attribute this to is perhaps unconscious feelings on the part of the actors that their music is no more than a necessary nuisance and not worthy of their full attention. And since many actors do not read music, I further assume they really can't tell if their music is playable or not.

Enough complaining—here comes the advice.

- Your music must be legible and properly prepared. If it isn't, do not expect anyone to be able to play from it.
- The lyrics and the melody line must be fully written out on your music. So-called "charts"—a sheet of music divided into the number of bars in the song with only the chord changes indicated—may be sufficient for jazz musicians and for your own accompanist, but they are next to useless for anyone else. It takes ten to fifteen minutes at most to

write down the lyrics on a piece of music. Why it is not done universally is beyond me. There is one major reason for having both the lyrics and the melody on the music page: if you forget the words or go off-pitch for any reason, the pianist can come to your rescue.

TRANSPOSITION

If you are singing a song that has been published, and you have the sheet music, and you do it in the published key, you are indeed fortunate. If you aren't so lucky, you will have to have your music specially prepared or doctored—transposed—to make it functional.

Published songs are usually in a key deemed either by the composer or someone at the publisher's office to be the easiest for a mass audience to deal with—even if it is different from the key the song was originally written or performed in. For example, in the Broadway production of the show *Funny Girl*, Barbra Streisand sang the song "People" in the key of A-flat. The published sheet music was transposed up to the key of B-flat, even though that put the song out of the range of a lot of singers. This was done because B-flat is considered to be an easier key than A-flat for amateur pianists. So if you've ever sung along comfortably with a recording, then purchased the sheet music and couldn't reach the high notes when the song was played on the piano, now you know why.

Every song can be transposed either up or down. With your accompanist or vocal coach try several different keys until you find the one that sounds and feels comfortable for your voice.

Many times people have walked over to the piano at an audition, handed their music to a pianist they were seeing for the first time and said, "Can you play this in a key I can sing it in?" What does the singer expect—that the pianist is Marvo the Magnificent Mind Reader? How could the pianist possibly know the singer's voice and which key would be suitable? Equally bad are those who say, for example, "Play 'As Time Goes By' in D-flat." I do agree that any pianist worth his salt should know any standard song like "As Time Goes By," and should be able to play it off the top of his head in most keys—but why leave anything to chance? Bring a copy of the music that has been prepared in advance—in your key—so the pianist can be comfortable playing for you, thus giving you the support you need and deserve.

Once upon a time, a pretty young woman approached the piano and gave me her music. It was the vocally demanding coloratura aria "Glitter And Be Gay" from *Candide* by Leonard Bernstein and Richard Wilbur. For anyone unfamiliar, it is a six-minute number containing many passages that push the abilities of even the most accomplished sopranos to their limits. It builds to a vocally demanding high E-flat—the fourth note from the end; possibly the only reason for doing this song at an audition is to show off that high E-flat. [NOTE: It should NEVER be done as an audition number! It is way too long, and too complicated. But I digress. On with the anecdote.]

Incredulously, I asked her, "Are you planning to sing the whole song?"

"Yes," she replied. "Can you play it?"

"Of course I can," I said.

She was halfway to the stage when she hurriedly came back to me and said, "I forgot to tell you—when we get to the ending, transpose it down a third."

If your music is to be transposed, have it fully written out in your key (see the section on Professional Copying which follows). However, this can be expensive, depending on the arrangement and number of pages; so it is permissible and quite common—but mind you, not as good as having the music fully written out—to have the transposed chords written over the measures. Keep the original chords visible—

don't scratch them out or use white-out—and have the transposed chords written in a different-color ink, usually red. That makes it easier for pianists to follow and play from.

Please remember that in preparing music that must be transposed, writing the new chords over the measures is the barest minimum you should have done. As I said before, never come in with the music in the original key and say, "Play it in C-sharp." It only takes ten to fifteen minutes at the most for a musician to write in the proper chords. Don't ever say there wasn't time to have it done.

Also—do not under any circumstances present music on which the original chords plus two sets of transposed chords are visible.

PROFESSIONAL COPYING

If your song follows the sheet music routine with almost no variation and is in the same key, then you really don't have to engage a professional copyist. But if your song is transposed, or if your arrangement is complicated, and you never plan to bring your own accompanist with you to auditions, you may find it beneficial to have your music specially prepared.

Professional copyists earn their living preparing music to order. Since the earliest days, music notation was done by hand, evolving into a craft practiced by skilled, trained "specialists" most often using pen and ink. No longer. The ubiquitousness of personal home computers has now put the craft of copying into the domain of anyone who can afford a computer and a music program. As much as this is anathema to most "hand" copyists, it is a godsend to you. You are sure to know someone with the ability to create publishable quality sheet music on his computer, personalized to your specifications.

If you do not know anyone who can do this work for you, look on the bulletin boards at rehearsal studios (some copyists put up their business cards), or look in the trade papers for advertisements. Or you can call a local music school or the American Federation of Musicians (the musician's union) office closest to where you live and ask for recommendations. Don't be embarrassed to request samples of the copyist's work before handing your song over; any reputable copyist will be pleased to show what he can do. And you must agree on the price beforehand!

The cost for this kind of work can be more than you might expect. Remember that if you are pursuing theatre as a career, you will have to make a monetary investment. Acting classes, dancing classes, vocal coaching are all examples of out-of-pocket expenses you readily understand and, probably, already budget for. Your music for singing auditions is, I think, an important part of your equipment, perhaps the most important. So if you amortize the cost of music preparation over the number of times you will use the song, it will be very inexpensive in the long run.

The musician's union has negotiated rates which are considered to be equitable minimum charges for music preparation. At the moment, there is no difference in price between hand copied or computer copied music (this is liable to change in the future). A competent pianist will be able to play from either type. Even if the person preparing your music is not a union member, the following prices will serve as a guideline as to what to offer: (NOTE: these rates are accurate as of this writing, in 1995. You can be assured that every year they will rise a bit to account for cost of living increases.)

- Transcribing (taking down a song from a tape where no music exists): $58.59 for the first 32 measures, and $35.16 for each additional page (of no more than 32 measures each). This includes the melody line, the lyrics, and chord symbols, effectively creating a "lead sheet." If you want a piano part created as well, expect to pay an *additional* $55.81 per page.
- Recopying per page (price includes the vocal line, the piano part, and the lyrics): $28.34. (NOTE: This price allows you to make multiple copies of your song.)
- Transposing adds a 50% surcharge to all the above prices.

THE CARE AND FEEDING OF YOUR MUSIC

Most of the pianos pianists have to play on in audition rooms, are, to put it nicely, not in the best of shape. Often there are several keys broken, and rarely are they in perfect tune.

Another practically standard feature of audition-room pianos is the lack of a proper stand for sheet music. Which is why a lot of the highly original ways people have of putting their music together simply don't work. It may be the piano's fault and not the actor's, but whatever the reason, it's mighty hard to play well for somebody when the music won't stay upright, or when it falls off the stand onto the keys, onto the pianist's lap, or onto the floor. And it does fall—with amazing regularity.

Sheet music you purchase from stores is printed on fairly sturdy paper—sturdier, anyway, than stationery or conventional bond paper. If you are going to use a photocopy of your music at an audition, it is better to have it reproduced onto a heavyweight stock—your music will stay in acceptable shape a lot longer. Remember, the music isn't staying at home, lying on your piano. It is being transported constantly, shoved in your dance bag or briefcase, and touched and played by many different hands. Regular bond paper wasn't designed to take that kind of abuse. Some neighborhood copy centers have on hand what is sometimes referred to as card-stock. Otherwise, you can take your music to one of several places that service the music industry. The cost of photocopying onto this kind of paper is usually between twenty-five and fifty cents a page.

Every pianist has the identical problem the first time playing through any piece of music: page turns. The pianist, all rumors to the contrary, is human, with only two hands. It is mighty difficult to turn a page of music while at the same time keeping the rhythm and the accompaniment going of a song he may not be overly familiar with. If your music is not the standard store-bought version, make sure it is printed on only one side of the page and accordion-folded as described below. This way, the music can be opened up flat and there will be no page turns to worry about. Four to five pages across will fit on most pianos.

Some people—especially some voice teachers—advocate placing each page of music between sheets of transparent plastic in a loose-leaf notebook. Certainly this presents a neat appearance, but consider these problems:

- The book is simply too cumbersome and heavy to carry around.
- The plastic covers tend to reflect light; because it is impossible to control the light source in an audition room, your music may be hard to read from.
- The plastic pages are hard to grasp. Pianists often inadvertently turn two pages at a time. Or the plastic sticks to the binder rings and the pages can't be turned at all.

Individual copies of your songs are a much better solution.

To be on the safe side, you should have a spare copy of your music tucked away at home. What if you lose your bag? What if you leave your music on the piano at the audition and can't remember later where it is? My personal collection of music grew significantly in this manner. Consider this a word to the newly wise.

Keep your audition songs in one place. Get a strong folder or envelope to store them in, sturdy enough to travel with. Do not put extraneous music in the portfolio, and do not remove any of the songs from the portfolio lest they not be there when you need them.

Please do not, for any reason whatsoever, fold your music in half. It just won't stay put even on a good music stand if it has been folded. Keep it flat.

The pages of your music must be attached. There are a lot of reasons why. I mentioned earlier about pages falling to the floor—so all

I'll add here is that I wish I had a dollar for every person who handed me their sheets of unattached music with a page missing, usually the last. "Oh, gosh, I'm sorry," they say. "I must have left that page at home." An all-too-obviously avoidable situation.

Never staple your music together. It is impossible to play from. Always tape your music.

TAPING YOUR MUSIC

It may sound incredibly picky, but there is a right way and a wrong way to tape music together. Since it is just as easy to tape it either way, please try the method I describe:

1. Let's assume you have a four-page song with music printed on only one side of each sheet. Take pages 1 and 2 and lay them flat on a table facing you, with page 2 to the right of page 1. The first trick here is to leave a small hairline space between the pages. This is to allow for the thickness of the tape when you fold the pages—the result is that the music folds flat and opens flat. Put tape down the front of the music only. Use three pieces of tape rather than one long one; if one piece splits down the center the other two are still there hanging in.

2. To attach page 3 requires a second trick. You put page 3 to the right of page 2, leaving the hairline space between the pages; but this time you attach the tape from the back side of the music only. This is so that when you fold the music, the sticky part of the tape is always on the inside of the fold.

3. Now as for page 4, place it to the right of page 3, leaving the space between the pages, and put the tape, once again, on the front.

4. You fold the music by leaving page 1 facing you on the front, with the other pages arranged accordion-style. Page 4 will face you on the back. Voilà, you're done.
5. If the song has five pages, for page 5 follow the instructions for page 3. If your music is longer than five pages, your song is too long.

Does any of this sound confusing? It'll all make lots of sense when you try your first one.

Interpretation: Acting the Song

This book will not go into the techniques of vocal production. That subject could fill a volume of its own. So what this part covers is not how to sing a song, but rather a discussion of how to perform a song.

In the words of stage Director (and former Casting Director and Theatrical Agent) Jeffrey Dunn, "Singing is acting on pitch." To elaborate in my own words, the very best singers act while singing; the two crafts are inseperable. Performing a lyric requires the same chops as is needed to perform a Shakespearean soliloquy plus the ability to do it on certain prescribed pitches—and in rhythm.

So you see, it's not enough to merely learn the words and the notes. You must completely understand what a song is saying and figure out how best to communicate its essence.

To do this, first make sure you understand the language and vocabulary of any song you sing. Although most lyricists strive to write in the vernacular, they occasionally use words which are decidedly not heard in everyday speech. Lyricist Ed Kleban used the adjective "peripatetic" in the song "One" (from *A Chorus Line*). Do you know what it means? What would you be saying if you were describing someone as having "imperturbable perspicacity" (from "Come Play With Me" by Stephen Sondheim from *Anyone Can Whistle*)? And what would you have been doing if you sang, "So I chaffed him and I gaily laughed" (from "Smoke Gets In Your Eyes," lyric by Otto Harbach, from *Roberta*)? If you sing these songs, you sure should make it your business to know what these words and lines mean!

And if any foreign words or phrases are part of the lyric, please not only know what they mean, but know how to pronounce them properly in their native language. Once upon a time at an audition a woman sang the title song from the 1960 Broadway musical, *Irma La Douce*. All eleven times she came to the titular line she pronounced it "Irma La Douche." The Director, a woman, was horrified and contemplated letting the auditioner know what she was doing wrong. But the Director decided against it, reasoning that as the girl probably performed this song many times at many different auditions, she would be humiliated once she learned of her error. So dear auditioner, if by chance you're reading these words...

Next take a look at the structure of the song. Is there a "verse"—a section which precedes the main melody? Verses are written to set up the song's subject matter. Often the main body of a song—the chorus—is written in general terms—a bid for widespread appeal. But the verse makes the song specific to a certain situation and can delineate a character. While verses are important lyrically, they are usually very simple and unmemorable musically. An almost singular exception to this is the haunting verse to Jerome Kern and Oscar Hammerstein's "All The Things You Are." Verses are almost always performed "freely," that is, not in tempo, with maximum attention given to the words. Underneath this, the pianist usually plays a minimal accompaniment, following the singer's lead.

Once you know the song's structure from a musical point of view, continue your analysis by treating the song as if it were a spoken monologue. If your song is from a show, read the entire script of the show. Make sure you define and understand the character who is singing the song to the point where you can answer the following questions: What prompts the character to sing at that point in the plot? What does the character hope to accomplish by delivering the message in the song? Is the character singing alone on stage (a soliloquy) or singing to another person? Does the character accomplish what he wants at the end of the song? What is the subtext of the song? (Subtext means the thoughts behind the words—sometimes very different from what is actually being sung.)

After you answer these questions for yourself, speak the lyric out loud as if it were a monologue. Do this a few times. Rephrase the song in your own words. Then sing it to the music—making sure you sing the lyric as clearly as if you were speaking it.

If you can't get the script, or the song was not originally created for a dramatic situation, make up a dramatic context for the song. Make the song into a scene (in your mind, of course), complete with scenery, costumes, and other characters (if necessary) and recreate this "scene" in your imagination when you audition.

Continuing your dissection of the song, find the natural phrases of the lyric and see how they rise or fall with the music. If you train yourself to think of song lyrics as a series of phrases, rather than as a sequence of individual words, your performance will be more natural. I always advise people to "sing the lyric," and not to be concerned with making pretty sounds at the expense of the meaning or intent of the song. Once you become aware of this technique, you will be able to instantly recognize which (famous) singers "sing the lyric," and which ones treat the words as merely sounds to put on pitch.

Never distort the English language as you sing by accenting the wrong syl*la*ble. Good songwriters are extremely careful to make the music and the lyric rise and fall as one, making the song sing as though it were dialogue. If the song you have chosen seems to force the language in places, you can usually bend the words back into their natural sound and compensate for the unevenness when you perform.

Look for the rhymes and make sure you rhyme them properly as you sing.

A question I get asked a lot is, "Where should I breathe?" There is a simple, all-purpose, all-inclusive answer to that: Always breathe with the lyric. Breathe when there is a pause in the thought. Look for punctuation marks, chiefly the commas and the periods. You can always take a breath wherever there is a period and, depending on the speed of the music, usually where there is a comma. And if you sometimes have to take a big breath and make it last a long time, it is probably unavoidable. The result of all this intellectualization of the breathing process is that your interpretation will sound intelligent.

Following my earlier suggestions about listening to recordings to find material, try to listen to more than one singer perform your song. It's not always possible, especially with obscure songs, but you'll be amazed at the different ways a song can be interpreted. As an exercise, listen to Stephen Sondheim's magnificent song "Send In The Clowns," from *A Little Night Music,* as performed by Glynis Johns on the original Broadway cast recording; by Jean Simmons on the original London cast recording; by Elizabeth Taylor on the movie soundtrack; by Angela Lansbury on a concert recording honoring Mr. Sondheim; and in the pop field by Frank Sinatra, Judy Collins, and Barbra Streisand. Each sings the same song with fairly similar arrangements, but there are worlds of difference in the nuances that these very talented performers find in the identical material, without any of them distorting the song's meaning.

Some of the music put in front of me at the piano has been heavily annotated with acting suggestions, such as "Open up here," "Think of all the people in this situation," "Look serious," and "Arms up." Although gestures can be expressive and effective, don't overdo them. They must be derived naturally. Nor while singing should you ever illustrate the various words or images in the song with your hands, as if performing for the hearing-impaired. Try to think in terms of the complete thought or the intent. If there is a particular word that conjures up a strong image, use a gesture to your advantage, but first understand what mood and effect the entire song is going after.

Wouldn't it be wonderful if you could move and sing at the same time? Standing like a statue just won't do. Find some movement that is natural, loose, and appropriate for the song you're singing. If you have a tendency towards stiffness—as in, "He is so wooden, if you light a match to him, he'll go up in flames"—get a friend who directs and/or choreographs to help devise some easy and effective movement for you. It could make all the difference. Do not do something choreographed either by your singing teacher or by your mother unless your mother is Agnes de Mille; it is sure to look amateurish. And, if you are working with a Director or Choreographer on your audition, do not, during a singing audition, do a heavily choreo-graphed song and dance number. If you begin performing something which looks too intricate, someone from the production team will probably say, "Don't move. Just sing." If the people sitting behind the desk want to see how well you dance, they will set up a specific dance audition at a separate time, where you will have to learn and perform specially prepared movements supervised by the show's Choreograph-er or Dance Captain.

To sum it up: Singing is merely a form of communication. Think of a song as a sung monologue. Acting (and moving) while singing is not as difficult as you may think it is if you aren't tense and uptight about it. If you understand what it is you want to communicate, you will find that the meaning, the breathing, and the movement will all fall into place naturally.

Working With a Vocal Coach

Don't confuse a vocal coach with a singing teacher. A singing teacher can help you with the actual production of sound, with breathing and support, and lots more technical advice. If you have vocal problems, or merely want to improve your technique, go to a singing teacher rather than a coach. You can find singing teachers through advertisements, through university music schools, through conservatories, or by recommendation (always the best way). The singer/comedienne Anna Russell quipped that "many of the world's greatest voice teachers [had] at one time or another ruined [her] voice." In the Don't-Let-This-Happen-To-You Department, try to get referrals from students before working with a teacher. Ask for credentials. Use common sense. And if you begin working with someone and you're not comfortable, you are not beholden to a contract. Go try someone else.

The vocal coach is used for guiding you in putting over your songs with maximum effectiveness. Although the coach may be able to help you technically, that generally is not his forté. At some point you will have to work with a coach to rehearse your material. Often, but not always, your accompanist (remember the accompanist you worked with to find material?) is also a vocal coach. Since anyone who plays the piano can call himself a vocal coach, there are several things to keep in mind so as to get the most for your money.

You should work with a coach who is also a pianist.

Your coach must be able to help you determine whether the music needs to be transposed and must have the skill to actually play the transposition. Then, he should be able to prepare your music so that anyone else can play it easily—even if your coach is not a professional copyist, at the very least he should be able to accurately write in the new (transposed) chords on your music. Be aware that some music you purchase may have inaccurate chords printed—your coach should be able to spot and correct the errors, so that when it is transposed, the chords are correct.

As I said before—and it bears repeating—it only takes ten to fifteen minutes at the most to write new chords on an existing song, so there's never any reason to say there wasn't time to get the song transposed. Lots of people use this excuse!

Your coach should tell you what key you are performing in. It makes you sound smart and knowledgeable to be able to say, "I do the song in the key of C and the music is in the correct key" or, "I'm doing this in E-flat, and the transposed chords are written in red ink"—instead of having to say, "I don't know what key I do this in. Isn't it on the music?" You don't even have to know what C or E-flat means. The pianist at the audition will know and you both will be more secure. Don't permit your coach to keep secrets from you.

Your coach should work out (with you) the musical introduction to the song, which will establish the pitch, allowing you to easily find your first note. Another true story: At one audition an actor gave me his music and, without saying a word, headed for the center of the room. I called him back. "What kind of introduction would you like?" I asked. "I don't know," he said. "what kinds of introductions are there?"

The answer to that question is there are many different kinds. From simple "bell" tones to arpeggiated chords to full four- or eight-measure piano solos. With your vocal coach, pick a simple, functional intro that will help you establish both the key and the mood for the beginning of the song. And make sure that it is written down so that any person playing your music will play the same thing. A common complaint I hear from singers is, "I had no idea what the pianist was playing for an intro. I couldn't find my first note." This is easily avoidable if the introduction you want is notated.

The ending as well as cuts or repeats should be clearly marked and indicated. Ditto for any tempo and dynamic markings. Some coaches charge extra for this service; some will charge according to their regular hourly rate. Remember that once the music is done properly, it is yours forever; so if the cost factor is amortized over the time you spend using the music, you'll find that it costs very little to have it prepared correctly.

Your coach should help you pick sixteen bars of your favorite audition song that makes a complete statement lyrically and musically. Why? Because of time restrictions at many auditions, you may be asked to sing only sixteen bars of a song. Plan for this in advance. If the top notes of your range are strong, you may want to select the part of the piece that contains the highest notes. Rehearse the sixteen-bar section complete with a short introduction and an ending as if it were an entire song. And mark the music so it is clear where the starting place and finish are for the abbreviated version.

Ask your coach to show you what changes have been made to the music so that you can coherently explain it to others. When I work with singers, I tell them specifically what to say regarding all of the above points, then we rehearse them. And don't accept a line from your accompanist like, "Don't worry, I'll always play for you." One day he won't be available and you'll be stuck. There's no reason in the world you shouldn't know everything about your music. Remember it is *your* music. Be intimately familiar with it.

Your coach should allow you to make a cassette tape of the accompaniments to your songs so that you can practice on your own. Don't ever work with someone who refuses to do this. You must practice your songs often, especially during the long periods between auditions. If you have songs on tape, you can always keep your material freshly prepared and stay in shape to sing without spending extra money for coaching every time there's an audition. And even if money isn't the problem, auditions are often arranged on very short notice and you might not be able to coordinate schedules with your coach or with your accompanist.

On the day of the audition make sure you run through your song at least once, preferably several times. To make sure there is no misunderstanding here, let me stress that at no time should your actual audition be the first time you sing on that particular day. When I auditioned four women for the leading role in a musical concert one showed up declaring that she hadn't warmed up and that she would sound better if she had. Well, how could the composer and I know how much better she would have sounded? We had no frame of reference for the quality of her voice. She did not get the role. Would she have gotten it if she had warmed up? Who knows. But she definitely would have been judged according to her performance-level qualifications.

If you happen to be doing a bit of traveling for the express purpose of auditioning (such as flying from one coast to another), please make sure that you build into your travel schedule adequate time for a music rehearsal, whether with a vocal coach or with a tape. Most often, the airfare and accommodations will be at your own expense. I strongly urge you never to undertake the financial inconvenience of a long-distance audition (or any audition for that matter) if you cannot prepare properly, and a coast-to-coast journey is no excuse for showing up without either music or vocal warm-up. Just your mere physical presence is not enough to ensure your getting hired. If you can't audition at your very best, don't ever schedule an appointment.

Performing

When to Bring Your Own Pianist

Because of monetary considerations the answer to this one depends to a great extent on how much the job means to you. Now I know that most people who try out for a job hope to get it as a result of the audition. So if this book is all about minimizing the risks and maximizing your effectiveness, my advice is that if you are auditioning for a featured role (as opposed to a chorus job) in a Broadway show or with a national touring company you should always bring your own pianist and find some way of working it out financially.

But I have to clarify that last statement a bit. The pianist you bring must be one with whom you have worked and who knows your material. I have seen more than one person come in to an audition with a pianist in tow and declare, "I just found out about this and only had enough time to call the pianist to get here in time. We haven't worked through the songs yet." As far as I am concerned, that is thrown-out money. The hired pianist winds up playing the music while seeing it for the first time, and usually ends up transposing at sight, the same as the staff pianist would. So there is no advantage for the performer.

Yes, I too have heard of auditions where the staff pianist was not up to snuff and word—and panic—spread among the hopefuls. This is the only case in which there is the slightest excuse for the situation in the previous paragraph; and this does not occur often. Most of the audition pianists, especially in New York, are skilled, talented, patient and experienced people who truly want you to look good.

I am aware that most people simply can't afford to spend the money to bring their own pianist every time they audition; which makes it inexcusable not to have one's own music in perfect condition so that it can be played easily by anyone at any time. But if you are auditioning with difficult or special material that has many changes of rhythm and tempo that demand perfect synchronization between the music and the voice, you must not expect any pianist, no matter how facile he is, to be able to give you the support that someone who knows the piece and has rehearsed it with you can.

In the mid-1970s I played piano for an Off-Broadway musical's auditions. One of the women scheduled to come in was slightly famous, but no one on the production team knew her except by having seen her previous work. They anticipated her audition. In their minds, she was exactly what they wanted for the role of the villainess, and so even before auditioning she had a better-than-average-chance of landing the role.

She brought in a song that she had sung in a flop musical on Broadway some years before. The song was unknown to me. The music was in manuscript, written in pencil and smeared, with no lyrics anywhere on the pages. A few tempo indications were barely decipherable, and there were several sets of chords above each measure—a sign that she (or someone else?) had performed this piece in several different keys.

But she had no idea which key was the most current, or even which key she wished to sing it in that day. She was used to having her own pianist, who knew all her music, come with her to auditions. She wasn't able to communicate anything to me before singing. "Just follow me," she said impatiently. I did—and badly. I couldn't read the music, and because there were no lyrics, I couldn't be sure we were ever in the same place at the same time. It was truly my most frustrating experience ever at the piano.

She compounded the felony by being exceedingly rude to me in front of the Director and Choreographer, degrading me and my abilities because I was unable to play her music properly. Needless to say, she brought nothing else with her to sing—"My pianist has all my music"—and the outcome was also unsurprising: she not only didn't get the part; her behavior negated any chance of a callback.

But given her pianist's unavailability, what should she have done under those circumstances?

She actually had several choices—all better than the one she picked. She could have tried to postpone or change her audition to a time when her own pianist would have been available. Or she could have found someone else with whom she could have worked beforehand to play for her. Or she could have found something simpler to sing. She also could have phoned me to suggest working with her the night before—her agent could have gotten my number from the Casting Director of the show. She is a talented lady and has worked, to great acclaim, on stage and screen since that unfortunate afternoon; so her subsequent auditions must've gone better.

It is imperative that the pianist you bring have a familiarity with the theatre and its customs.

For the original production of *The Most Happy Fella* in 1956, the chorus people were auditioned as if they were solo artists. Every prospective chorus member had to come in and do a classical operatic aria in either French or Italian and also do something in English. A woman brought her own accompanist, a little old lady, to the 46th Street Theatre where the auditions were being held. The woman went to the Stage Manager and asked, "Where does my accompanist go?" The Stage Manager said, "She has to go downstairs and then underneath the stage to the orchestra pit. The piano is underneath the stage." So the little old lady followed the directions and went to the pit.

The woman began singing "Amour! Viens aider ma faiblesse" from *Samson et Delilah*. Not too long into the aria, Frank Loesser, composer of *The Most Happy Fella*, called out from the audience, "Stop, stop, stop! Please tell your piano player that she's playing too loud. I cannot hear you."

The woman leaned over the stage and said to the little old lady, "Violet, you're playing too loud. Would you soften it down, please."

The woman started singing again, and this time the piano was deafening.

Frank Loesser came down the theatre aisle, leaned over the orchestra pit rail, and said, "Violet, you're playing too loud!" From underneath the stage, Violet yelled back, "Do you want a finger up your @$%, Bud?"

Advice to the Personal Accompanist

Please remember that you are there as an accompanist. You are not auditioning—or rather, you shouldn't be auditioning at the same time as the person who brought you.

This may sound strange, but sensational piano playing at an audition is distracting. The attention and focus must be placed squarely on the singer. Keep your accompaniments simple, straightforward, and supportive, and you will be doing your job well.

If the audition atmosphere is relaxed enough to permit some dialogue between the singer and the director, it is customary for the singer to introduce you; otherwise, you usually remain nameless. It comes with the territory.

However, if you hear that a piano job is available on the show, it is permissible to let your interest be known by giving your résumé to the stage manager, or whoever is checking people in at the audition. If they are interested, they will get in touch and arrange for you to audition for the proper people.

Singing the Right Kind of Song

So you now have a potent—and full—song portfolio. How do you know which songs to sing for which audition?

As all of you who have done your "history of the musical theatre" homework know, up until the late 1960s nearly every musical written for Broadway had a similar "sound." Broadway was a fertile source of popular music, producing a steady and seemingly unending stream of "hit-parade" songs for a solid 50 years. Record companies vied with each other for the privilege of backing shows, in order to win the potentially lucrative rights to record the original cast albums of the shows. But this changed drastically during the 1960s. Popular music shifted radically in the direction of "rock 'n' roll" while Broadway continued with its tried-and-true formulae.

Thankfully, now, in the 1990s, Broadway plays host to a roster of shows with a wide variety of musical sensibilities. This presents a challenge to the auditioner: you must be aware of the style of the music in the show for which you are auditioning. Is it contemporary? Pop-opera? Rock? Traditional? Operetta? Country-Western? A revival? Each would have very different types of music and therefore different requirements for singers.

Under ideal conditions, pick a song that is in the same period and style as the show. Don't make yourself crazy trying to match the score exactly. All I want to bring to your attention is that if you are auditioning for a traditional Broadway musical, it won't do you much good to sing a song written by the Rolling Stones. Or if you are auditioning for a show with a Country-Western-flavored score, it is inappropriate to sing a Victor Herbert aria. It's common-sense time.

If your song portfolio consists of a number of different songs from several styles and periods, you won't ever be in the upsetting position of having to learn a new song instantly because you have just gotten an audition for which you don't have anything suitable.

Jerry Herman cautions: "Don't learn a new song for each audition. The best auditions I have listened to are by people who have been doing the same material for years and years. There's nothing that can replace the comfort of a song that you have been singing and feel secure with. So many people who came to the *La Cage aux Folles* auditions prepared something French or something they thought had a French sound, not realizing that we just wanted to hear their voices. Don't underestimate the imaginations of the people who are sitting out there in the dark. They really only need to hear what sounds best on you."

Barry Moss advises, "Once you have a song that works, stick to it. Even if you've sung it dozens of times, the people auditioning you are hearing you do it for the first time. In the beginning of her career Carol Burnett sang the same song for years and it took her very far." (For the record, it was "Everybody Loves to Take a Bow" from *Hazel Flagg*.)

If your agent is the one who is arranging the audition, your agent should be the one who lets you know something about the style of the show, and if the production team wants you to prepare anything special. If you get to the audition and find out that you have not been properly briefed, it is your responsibility to raise hell with whomever set up your appointment. You have the right to be adequately informed. If it is indeed your agent who is at fault, don't let it happen more than once; change your agent as soon as possible.

ROCK MUSICALS

In 1969, when the show *Hair* opened, a complete score for a Broadway show incorporated the "new" sound of rock for the first time. Because *Hair* was a runaway success, the door was flung wide open to other attempts to (sometimes uneasily) fuse contemporary sounds in music with theatrical subject matter.

Because rock music is so stylistically different from standard "Show music" auditioning for rock musicals requires special preparation. Joseph Church, the Musical Director and supervisor for all companies of *The Who's TOMMY* counsels: "The difficulty in finding good rock audition material stems from two sources. First is a customary failure on the part of the production when setting up the auditions to specify the rock style. 'Rock 'n' roll' and 'rock' have evolved into very broad terms, and so the category 'rock musical' has become a generic distinction. Nonetheless the terms continue to be used to describe all sorts of musicals which incorporate popular music forms. The onus therefore falls on the performer and coach to determine the appropriateness of a piece of material for a particular audition. One does not sing Sondheim for a *My Fair Lady* audition; similarly, one should avoid 'Crocodile Rock' while singing for *Jesus Christ Superstar*. The material appropriate for an audition should match the specific rock style of the show. For *TOMMY*, for example, a good selection would be hard rock, a song with dramatic content in the lyric and a broad melodic range, similar to the style of Pete Townshend and *TOMMY*. For *Grease*, obviously, an emotional fifties pop ballad in 12/8 time will probably fill the bill. Like any other musical style in the theatre, rock takes many forms, and it is wise for the performer to be as aware of and proficient in as many of them as possible.

"The second problem in choosing rock audition material is inherent in the music itself. The majority of rock music consists of repetitive, often banal melodies, rhythmic feels which cannot be easily reproduced at a piano, a large proportion of instrumental interludes, and lyrics which are screamed unintelligibly, probably in order to mask their meaninglessness. Certainly none of these qualities is desirable in an audition song, which should have a strong dramatic point of view, a melody which shows off the voice, and can be accompanied by a piano. To a certain extent, some of the drawbacks of rock music are accepted by Directors and Music Directors as unavoidable. Nonetheless, it is highly advantageous to seek out rock material that does have a strong melody, does not have three measures of rest for the singer after each measure of melody (e.g. the verse of Elton John's 'Don't Let The Sun Go Down On Me'), has a playable accompaniment, and, above all, a dramatic and actable lyrical content. Music of this description does exist in abundance. Good places to start looking would be The Beatles, Billy Joel, and Paul Simon, but there are many, many others."

At the Audition:
Do's and Don't's, Hints and Secrets

Here's the only irrefutable rule of auditioning:
If you are auditioning for a musical, you must always bring your own music.
I can't stress this strongly enough. Many years ago, I coached someone for his audition for the original production of *Barnum*. The performer also engaged me to play for him at the audition itself.

At the Edison Theatre, where the auditions were being held, about thirty-five youngish men sat in the first few rows. The first man was called. He stepped onto the stage, conferred with the pianist, then went over to center stage and sang "Happy Birthday."

"You didn't bring any music with you?" asked Joe Layton, the Director.

"No," replied the actor.

The second guy was called, and surprisingly the exact same process was repeated.

Mr. Layton stood up and said, "How many of you don't have your own music?"

More than half of those present raised their hands.

So Mr. Layton had to make his choices after hearing about twenty actors in a row sing, "Happy Birthday."

Okay. Let's keep things in perspective. That's not such a terrible anecdote. The world didn't come to an end. Mr. Layton didn't run out of the Edison Theatre screaming and immediately quit the business. *Barnum* wasn't canceled or postponed until those auditioning could return with obscure show songs.

And as far as I was concerned, this story had a happy ending: My friend—who did not sing "Happy Birthday" but, rather, sang an obscure song we prepared and rehearsed (What did you expect him to sing with me coaching him?)—was chosen for the show and played in it throughout its New York run.

But I would bet a substantial sum of money that had all the auditioners prepared songs, a slightly different group of them would have made telephone calls to their families saying they were cast in a Broadway show.

More perspective now.

The above occurrence was a rarity. Most people who audition for musical shows in New York know they should prepare a song and bring the music. Although the number of unenlightened performers makes the previous case noteworthy, it was not an isolated happening. I have sat at the piano during many other auditions at which at least one person came up to the piano stating, "I didn't know I had to bring music." Always carry music with you, especially if you're not sure.

But lest you think that not bringing music is an error committed by only novice performers, consider what happened when a Famous Television (Sitcom) Actress auditioned to replace Bernadette Peters in the Broadway production of *Into The Woods*. Walking in empty-handed (no music) she announced that she was more of a jazz-singer than a show-singer. But—if they wanted to hear her voice, she would be willing to sing "It Had To Be You." Without missing a beat she turned ever so slightly in the direction of the accompanist and said "Find me." Then she started singing a capella. Unfortunately, she was singing in the cracks of the keys (rather than on exact pitch) so the pianist had difficulty "Find"-ing her. When she finished, with the utmost courtesy the production team asked her if she could sing something else, possibly something from a show. She said she could do "Adelaide's Lament" from *Guys and Dolls*. Once again, with no eye contact, she snapped "Find me" to the pianist. This time he was ready, but no less annoyed. Needless to say, this Famous Actress did not make her Broadway debut in *Into The Woods*. But this story has become a classic show-biz joke, and having been often retold in the eight years since this event happened it has had a far longer run than the show itself.

If you come to an audition and for whatever reason don't have music, don't ever sing a cappella. It is extraordinarily difficult to stay on pitch without the aid of a musical instrument. There has never been a justification good enough to warrant it. If your music is unavailable, it is best to attempt to reschedule your audition to a time when you can bring the music. If you insist on signing a cappella, the only thing you will accomplish is writing off the audition. You might as well stay home.

The staff pianist provided by the production company is also a very important eyewitness to the audition process. He can be impartial and objective about the proceedings because he doesn't make casting decisions and most often isn't even privy to the production team's discussions.

Thus the pianist's observations can be trenchant and should be taken very seriously. One especially accomplished pianist (who shall remain anonymous) incisively noted that "Endless numbers of people, one after another, follow the exact scenario as if there were only one way to do an audition: They walk into the room, humiliate the pianist, take their spot in the center, tell what song they're going to sing, who the writers are, what show it's from, bow their heads with intense concentration, give the pianist a Nazi nod and then do a standard version of their song untouched by brains—and hope we make them a star."

What is meant is that an audition is not a classroom situation; it is the real world. You don't have to please a teacher. Although you need to be thoroughly prepared, you must not appear to be mechanically so.

Here is a list of "Audition Do's and Don't's," with accompanying explanations:

1. No matter how unimportant the job may seem at the time, always take auditions seriously. Always do your best. You never know what's going to happen in the future. Some people have long memories, and some have short. Assume that the people you audition for fall into the former category.

At the auditions for the anthology of Stephen Sondheim's work, *Putting It Together*, a singer with several recordings to her credit stated "You know, I'm primarily a recording artist and would feel more comfortable singing to a track." The Musical Director countered by saying, "This is a live show and we're going to be performing it live, so I'd appreciate it if you'd sing with a live accompaniment." The singer replied, "I don't really know why I'm here. I don't do shows." She then did sing live, to a live piano accompaniment, "Don't Rain On My Parade." As good as she is, that song did not allow her to be heard in any way other than in (unfavorable) comparison to Barbra Streisand. So off she went, presumably to resume her recording career.

2. No matter what else you've had to do before the audition, pull yourself together somewhere outside of the place where the auditions are being held. Always remember that you are in a spotlight from the moment you are seen by any member of the production team of the show. If you walk into the room, or even the audition area, dishevelled and "spacey," it will be difficult later on to erase that first impression.

3. Auditions are notoriously off-schedule. You will most likely have to wait for some period of time before you are called. Instead of sitting there worrying, there are several things you can do to pass the time: Go over the songs you plan to sing, read a book, do a crossword puzzle—anything to help relieve the anxiety. Often you will know some of the others whose scheduled audition times are just

before or just after yours, so you can spend a pleasant few minutes chatting with old friends or making new ones.

4. An important question to ask the person who checks you in is, "For whom will I be auditioning?" By asking this, you will know how many people you will be facing—the number can vary from one person to as many as a dozen or so—and which members of the production team will be present. You are well within your rights to know this information. The roster of people will change with every audition. For musicals, there will most often be a Director, a Choreographer, a Musical Director—who either will conduct the orchestra or play the piano during performances—and a Producer, more than likely, several. When you audition for a new show in New York, you can expect the Writers to be present. In some cases there will be assistants, friends, wives, husbands, and even lovers of the various aforementioned participants.

5. Leave your disappointments and anxieties outside the audition area. At the chorus auditions for the original production of *The Music Man*, one fellow came in and sang his sixteen bars. As with everybody else, the late Director, Morton DaCosta, didn't have time to say anything but "Thank you very much." The actor walked down to the footlights and said, "That's easy for you to say, you son-of-a-bitch!" and harangued Mr. DaCosta for several minutes until he was dragged off the stage. Obviously the actor was frustrated by several failed auditions. You must, to the best of your ability, leave all of that behind and forget the ogres who are out front. Your attitude must "read" success, not failure.

6. Have your music—and your picture and résumé—ready in your hands before entering the room; don't search through your bags while everyone waits.

7. Figure out what you are going to sing before you enter the audition room. You'll be a lot calmer if you have that planned ahead of time. Fairly frequently the Director asks what songs you have brought with you, and after you rattle off the list, he may ask you to sing something other than what would have been your first choice. If the decision is yours, sing your most exciting song first; as if you were only going to sing one number.

A man, auditioning for the original Broadway production of Stephen Sondheim's *Passion*, sang his first song, a ballad, impressively. The Musical Director requested another song. The singer asked "Would you like an up-tempo or a patter song?" The Musical Director replied, "Just sing something contrasting." The singer and the pianist conferred and frantically flipped through the auditioner's music. Quite obviously, the singer didn't have a clear idea of what he wanted to do for his second number. He asked the Musical Director "Do you want a more pop sound or a more legit sound?" Patiently, the M.D. replied "Just sing something different. You choose." The singer and the pianist again flipped through his music. Confused, the singer queried the Musical Director, "Should it be comedic or dramatic?" The M.D. took up the challenge and made a decision: "Sing me a Country-Western song!" The singer did not have a Country song but realized that at this point he couldn't argue with the M.D. In a last-ditch effort to save face he did "Stars" from *Les Misérables* with a country twang, the pianist improvising the appropriate accompaniment. Are you surprised to learn that the singer did not get a callback? I was assured that he would have, had he sung the right second song.

Make sure that you are familiar and comfortable with whatever music you bring with you to the audition. If you don't bring the music to a song you performed only once ten years ago, and whose words you don't really remember all that well, you won't be tempted to use it if you're asked to sing an additional song.

8. Take the same advice your mother gave you before a long car trip: Use the rest room before you are called in to perform.

9. When you enter the audition room, try not to come in with all your personal belongings—if you have a coat, a dance bag, a purse, and a spare pair of shoes, you immediately convey a bag-person image. It is usually possible to leave your things in the waiting area and ask one of the other people auditioning to keep an eye on them while you are inside. If you must bring your bags and coat in with you, place them right beside the door so they can be grabbed quickly on your way out—it makes for the swiftest and most graceful exit. Do not under any circumstances place your things on the same table the Director uses. Don't laugh, people have done that! If the audition is on a stage, leave your things at the proscenium arch, and, if possible, out of sight of the audience.

10. When you are ushered into your performing area, your name will be announced and, if you have not brought your own pianist, you should proceed directly to the piano. If you have brought your own accompanist, he should go to the piano and you should go to your performance space. Sometimes you will be introduced to the people observing the audition, sometimes not. If you are not personally introduced, don't ask "Who are you?" of anyone. If you didn't ask outside, you can question the staff pianist about who is who.

11. Don't try to engage the Director or writers in "icebreaker" conversation. Although you would be trying to be charming and friendly—and attempting to ease your own nerves before you sing— it rarely comes off quite that smoothly. It can even backfire on you. When the legendary late George Abbott was a mere 99 years old, he directed a production of *Damn Yankees* at the Paper Mill Playhouse in New Jersey. Mr. Abbott was looking through the pictures and résumés when a pleasant woman entered the room and addressed him. "Hello, Mr. Abbott, I was in five of your shows. Do you re-

member me?" she asked brightly. Mr. Abbott looked up, glanced at the woman and replied, "No!" Speaking to the production team can be unwittingly intrusive, counterproductive, and, in truth, just slows things down. I know it sounds harsh, but the rule "Don't speak unless you're spoken to" seems to be a good one to follow.

12. Sometimes someone on the production team will ask "So what are you going to sing for us?" just to break through those first awful moments when you are on your most formal behavior. In this case, it is OK to clue them in, but unless specifically asked, don't announce your song choice as if you were at an elementary school recital.

13. Know who wrote the song you will sing, but don't tell anyone unless asked. If you do say in advance what you are going to sing do not also recite the song's source-show and authors as if the additional information were part of the title. Assume that your listeners already know. The more professional the audition situation, the more likely the casting team will know almost every show song ever written. (Yes, of course, if they ask you more questions about the song, which may happen if you're singing something particularly obscure, you may answer.) Would you believe that some people who sing a song they heard on a singer's compilation album automatically think that the singer has written the song as well? More than one woman has confidently stated that the song she was going to sing from the album of timeless standards (penned by some of the greatest songwriters of this century), "Lush Life," was written by the album's singer, Linda Ronstadt.

14. Do your audition full-out. Don't hold back on your energy or enthusiasm. Those actors who "perform" their auditions rather than just "singing" them seem to get the callbacks.

15. Don't come in challenging the production team's casting predisposition–especially in a confrontational manner. The supporting role of the tempestuous diva, Carlotta, in the original Broadway production of *The Phantom of the Opera* ultimately brought Judy Kaye the Tony Award. But another gifted lady performer with a versatile voice came in to audition for that role, really wanting to play the leading role of Christine. She strode out on the stage and tried to locate the show's Director, Harold Prince, who was sitting with the other creative personnel in the darkened theatre. "Hal! Hal!," she called, "I know you think of me as the diva but I'm really a lot younger than you think. I want you to consider me for Christine." Mr. Prince, put on the spot, declined. The lady pushed a bit more. The Director got a bit testy. And to date, this lady who probably would have been a terrific Carlotta has not played either role in any of the many productions of *Phantom* around the world.

And for heaven's sake, don't offer any sob stories to the production staff. One woman always came in with a story on the order of "I really have to do this show because my son is going to college in the fall and I need the tuition." Let's not even be so cynical as to doubt the veracity of her story. But nobody will hire her out of sympathy. Her remarks always provoked the opposite reaction—I heard the comments made after she left the room. They were not full of warmth and compassion. It's much better to let your talent do the talking.

Excuses, Excuses, Excuses

All of you who think you are being original when you offer an explanation as to why you are not at your best at an audition, please think again. Every possible excuse has been offered too many times. And they are incredibly self-defeating. I'd be filthy rich if I had a dollar for every time the following had been said:

I have a cold.
I have just recovered from a cold.
I feel a cold coming on.
I didn't have any music to sing so I just stopped at the
    music store and bought this song. How does it go?
I just found out about the audition this morning so I
    couldn't prepare adequately.
My pianist has my music.
I'm not warmed up.
I had a long night (rough night, heavy gig, hot date, etc.)
    last night.
I just got into town.
I'm in the process of moving—or, I have just moved—
    so my music isn't in good shape.
I learned this song from the record, but I never heard the
    accompaniment before.
It's too early to sing—my voice isn't warmed up.
    (Said at every audition held before noon.)

Please note that a once-popular excuse is not heard much anymore: "My dog chewed up my music." I don't know whether the disappearance of this excuse means that more actors have cats than have dogs, or maybe there are just better-trained canines around.

16. If you arrive later than your appointed time, it is usually unnecessary to offer any kind of excuse for your lateness. Everyone is aware of the unpredictability of public transportation and the unreliability of taxicabs in city traffic. It's not uncommon for actors to be seen in an order different from the planned schedule. If many people are auditioned in a day, the Director and his cohorts are usually not aware that you are late until you tell them. I don't mean to condone lateness, but if you find yourself unavoidably late, just be composed when you enter the room and say nothing.

17. If the audition is in a room, rather than a theatre, pick a spot to sing from that is near—but not right next to—the piano, a comfortable distance away from the people watching. That distance is of utmost importance because it allows those observing to approximate the way you would look onstage. Since you will want to move a bit while you sing, as opposed to standing like a statue, do so laterally— sideways.

Do not creep forward. Moving toward the casting team can intimidate them and make them uncomfortable, if not downright frightened. One man, upon reaching the final chorus of the Gershwin song "There's a Boat Dat's Leavin' Soon for New York" from *Porgy and Bess*, rushed forward toward the table at which sat the Director, Choreographer, et. al. At the song's climax he leapt on top of the table, where he finished, expecting that he had created a memorable impression. The team certainly remembered not to hire him. He took a chance, but the wrong one. (And a dangerous chance it was, for the table could have broken...)

18. If you are in a theatre this next point is not a concern, but in a studio you have to be aware of what your eyes focus on while you sing. Most people advise you not to look directly at the people auditioning you so as not to challenge them with the lyrics to the song. You should focus on a spot just over their heads. But pick at least one short phrase that can be sung right to one of the members of the casting team. The phrase should be informational in content—not something that

threatens or requires either a verbalized "answer" or an (emotional) response from the listener.

19. Don't use props while you audition. Even depending on a chair to be present can cause problems in some audition rooms, and also takes time to set up. It is very important for the Director to see how you use your body when you sing, so sitting in a chair somewhat defeats the purpose. Don't depend on the piano to lean on or refer to. What if your audition is on a stage and the piano is in the pit? It's better to stay as self-contained as possible. And as flexible as possible.

Speaking of props, there was a young man who came to auditions carrying his rather large teddy bear. He never let go of the bear and even held it close to him when he sang. But the bear was never referred to in the guy's song. Once, the Director was grouping people by type and this young man was one of ten lined up—only to the Director's surprise there were eleven faces in the row.

20. If the Director suddenly asks you to perform your song in a manner different from the way you are used to, don't challenge him or resist. Make an honest attempt to follow the instructions, even if you think you look or sound foolish. The Director is trying to see how adaptable you are and how speedily you can absorb new ideas. You will get additional brownie points if you show you are willing to go out on a limb.

21. Don't ask the question "Do you want me to sing two songs?" either before or after you do your first one. Everyone in the room assumes you have brought more than one, so the best procedure is to pause after your first song and wait for some response. Either you will be asked to sing something else or you will be told something like "Thank you, that song showed us everything we needed to hear," in which case you should politely make preparations to leave the room. Don't put them on the spot. The remark that sounds like a brush-off may not be. Most trained listeners can tell after the first six-

teen bars how well you sing, and one song may indeed be sufficient for them to determine whether or not you fit in with the specific needs of the show.

22. It is highly unlikely for the production team to offer you a job on the spot. If they didn't think you were right for their show they will be polite. And if they are wild about you their reactions will most likely be muted. If they are enthusiastic it doesn't necessarily mean that they will hire you, and if they are ambivalent and not very enthusiastic it doesn't necessarily mean they won't. Since there is no way to know for sure, you must leave the audition area with grace and composure. Then you get on with your life.

How to Talk to the Pianist and What to Say

If you are not bringing your own accompanist, the staff pianist provided by the production is—usually—your only friend in the audition room. Having been hired by the production company specifically to work for you, the pianist will come through with flying colors, if you provide the basic professional courtesies. Broadway's most experienced audition pianist, Sande Campbell, hopes to be "treated as an artistic partner so we can make theatrical magic happen in that dull room."

Your interaction with the pianist is a dead giveaway as to your experience level. Sometimes this isn't a bad thing. But in a professional situation appearing to be an amateur is not desirable. If the pianist suspects your amateur standing, he will have to play differently for you: more carefully, more ready to cover you on the melody, more prepared to bail you out in case of problems, and less likely to dare to be creative.

One thing that will immediately red-flag you is if you put your music in front of the pianist and ask "Are you familiar with this?" What you are really saying is that you have just recently learned this particular song and it's very existence is new to you. The pianist is a musician who is particularly knowledgeable in the field of theatre music. The chances are good that not only does he know the song, but has most likely played it at innumerable other auditions over the years, as well as probably having played pit piano for a production of the show it is from at some point in his career. Always assume that the pianist knows the material. If he doesn't, he can certainly read music, and, in fact, has been hired for his ability to play whatever is put in front of him. Familiarity with your particular song does not assure you that the pianist will play it any better or worse.

The only thing that can assure you of the pianist's ability to support you satisfactorily is the proper preparation of your material. No pianist, no matter how accomplished, can be expected to be a mind reader and correctly guess at what is not written down, for example, the tempo and feeling of your song.

Even if the audition is running behind, you will be allowed a few moments to give the pianist a clear idea of the tempo by softly singing a few measures of the song to him at the speed you wish to perform it. If you are performing, say, "You Gotta Have Heart" from *Damn Yankees*, it is very likely that you will do it at the standard tempo expected for the song, so just saying that you do that way is sufficient. If your music is legible and transposed, and the introduction, ending, tempo changes, and any dynamic markings are clearly indicated, you will not need more than about twenty seconds to confirm the routine and point out any tricky spots. Broadway's esteemed Musical Director, Paul Gemignani, counsels to use your limited audition time auditioning rather than in giving instructions and explaining complicated routines to the pianist.

Now I can't stress this next point strongly enough:
The staff pianist already has his job; don't make him audition his skills for you.

Singers trying out for the original Broadway production of *The Phantom of the Opera* brought in operatic material. Fair enough. But several had the audacity to put full orchestral scores of *Wozzeck* and *Lulu* on the piano. On this occasion the pianist was the amazingly talented Scott Frankel and he credibly sight-read (creating a playable piano part from) the full scores. I guarantee that the pianist at your audition will not be as good as Mr. Frankel, so don't ever ask the pianist to play from full orchestral scores!

And in the Compassion Department, don't treat the pianist as a human extension of the piano. Remember the old barroom sign, "Please don't shoot the piano player—he's doing the best he can"? The audition pianists really do try to support you properly. They do a yeoman's work in accompanying sometimes up to a hundred people a day, especially considering the horrendous state of most of the music they must play from. Before you leave the area, please be courteous and say, "Thank you" to the pianist. Take it from me, everyone in the room will notice.

To sum up, these are the four things to tell the pianist:

1. The key
2. Where to start
3. Where to stop
4. How fast to play

What to Do if You Forget the Lyrics

In two words: Keep calm. It happens more often than anyone realizes. Maybe in one out of every ten auditions. It is not the end of the world. Naturally no one would ever wish for it to happen, but if it does, your aplomb in dealing with it can turn what seems like a disaster into quite a victory for you.

Once again, don't try to make excuses. They are not necessary and almost always make you look bad.

Don't make an issue of it. Don't comment on it. The casting team is aware enough that you forgot the lyric, you don't have to hammer it home. Just find your place and keep going.

Most often, people forget lyrics when they aren't fully concentrating on what they are doing. Don't let your mind wander, no matter how many times you have performed that particular song. Keep it fresh.

But if you should suddenly go blank and can't remember what word comes next, you can simply turn to the pianist, who will throw you the lyric so you can continue. If the lyrics are not on the music, that truly is a disaster, and you should immediately go back to the section entitled "How to Prepare Your Music" and memorize it.

Even singing la-la-la is all right until you remember the words— if it is a short lapse. Listen to Judy Garland singing "You Go To My Head" on her live "Judy at Carnegie Hall" album. Yes, Judy Garland forgot the lyrics. A big star. At Carnegie Hall, yet. And preserved forever on a best-selling phonograph record. But she handled it with her marvelous sense of humor. Brilliantly.

You can, as Judy did, sing anything over the notes. If you think quickly on your feet and are entertaining enough, after a few moments no one will remember your gaffe.

The Open Call

The first professional audition most people encounter will probably be an "open call"—commonly referred to as a "cattle call." At this time you will be one of hundreds competing for the chance to get your foot in the door. "Open call" means just that—it is open to anyone who wishes to be seen and considered.

In the case of a Broadway show, periodic open calls are required by Actors' Equity. If you are not yet in the union, you probably will have to stand on a long line in order to put your name on a lengthy list of contenders and will not be seen until after all the members of Equity and those who are "Equity Eligible" are seen. Sometimes, before even getting a chance to sing, actors are "typed out"—that is, only those who have the right look for the show are asked to stay. A frustrating situation, but don't let it discourage you. Keep going to these kinds of auditions; eventually you will be allowed to show your stuff.

Open calls are not the most anticipated part of the auditioning process for the production team. The "top brass" is rarely present at these events; usually the Stage Manager, or the Assistant Director, and the Dance Captain preside. Since the people who listen to the hoards of hopefuls do not want their time spent in vain, they are hoping to discover new talent. Those performers who make a good impression will be remembered, their résumés kept on file, and then one day if the situation warrants it, be asked to sing for the real decision-makers.

Unfortunately, because the performers who show up at the open call are not pre-screened, either by agents or Casting Directors, there is a high level of amateurishness and unprofessional behavior. Joseph Church remembers: "The open call for *TOMMY* brought out, not surprisingly, every rock 'n' roll wannabe and shouldneverbeallowed-tobe within a hundred mile radius. One very sincere auditioner held index cards to remember the lyric of his song choice. 'See me,' he sang, and looked down at the cards. He continued, 'Feel me,' and looked down at the cards again. 'Touch me,' and he looked down again. 'Heal me.' We assumed he had these eight words memorized for their repetition in the second verse, but we were wrong. Again he looked down at his index cards and sang, 'See me,' and looked down again, 'Feel me,' looked down again, and so on. Four verses worth."

Because of the sheer numbers of people who show up to be auditioned at an open call, you will rarely be permitted to sing an entire song. Instead, you will usually be asked to sing a portion (eight to sixteen bars) of any song with which you are familiar and comfortable. An accompanist is almost always provided.

Follow the instructions precisely! Don't ask the accompanist to do more than sixteen bars, even if the song is very fast or very short. He is bound by the same time constraints you are, and must carry out the wishes of the production staff. If you are requested to sing a ballad, don't do an up-tune, and vice versa. Of course, you should be able to perform the whole song all the way through if you are asked—but only if you are asked!

Don't be put off if you have to sing in front of the others auditioning. Because of time considerations, it is sometimes more expedient to keep everyone in the audition room while one by one you are called upon to perform. This often happens in professional dance calls. It is an uncomfortable situation, but remember that everyone feels the same way and the production staff is aware of it. But the performers who appear the most fearless and who do the best under the pressure will have an edge over the competition.

Although—as you know by now only too well—I have gone through great pains to convince you to perform little-known material, in the open-call situation it is not vitally important to knock yourself out finding an obscure song. You may sing something well-known.

What matters most is to make the best impression you can as quickly as possible. Sing something that shows off your vocal prowess; and if you look right and sound right, and display a high standard of professionalism, you will stand out.

Summer Stock

If you are auditioning for a part in a summer stock production, it is essential that you familiarize yourself with the show—or shows, if you are auditioning for the whole season of productions the theatre is doing. As you read in an earlier chapter of this book, before you audition you should find out what the roles in the shows require in terms of age, look, and type, as well as what songs those characters sing.

Along with your standard audition material, you should prepare the songs sung by the characters for which you want to be considered. Again, it's worthwhile to restate that in the current economic situation, most summer stock theaters or dinner theaters are struggling financially; so it is folly on your part to audition for the role of, say, Lois Lane in *Kiss Me, Kate* if you are a soprano. The theaters simply do not have the money to transpose the leased orchestrations, let alone have the songs rescored, no matter how much they may want you in their production.

You should have prepared not only the actual show songs, but also at least one song that is similar to the real songs. Don't sing from the actual shows unless you are sure the team wants you to. When you get to the audition, ask the person who checks off your name when you arrive what the casting team is requesting. This way you can be mentally prepared and you won't have to ask once you are in the room. If the person outside doesn't know, when you are inside ask the pianist what others have been doing. If you've taken my advice, you'll be ready either way.

You'll be in an especially good position if you interest the production team when you sing a song of your choosing, and then are asked to sing from the show. If you have readied the show song beforehand, you could secure yourself the part in those few minutes.

Most summer stock theaters and dinner theaters do fairly standard-fare presentations, so the libretti and scores—as well as recordings—are widely available in libraries and theatre book stores.

Once again, there's no substitute for preparation. You'll have an edge over those unprepared.

At the Callback

Final casting decisions are never made in the first round of auditions. During that time, the people doing the casting are making special note of anyone who could possibly fill the roles in the show. These actors are given a "callback"—which is just another chance to audition on a different day. Most often the callback is scheduled within a week of the first audition. However, there have been cases of callbacks being scheduled months later. If you have been selected for a return visit, it means that you are under serious consideration. Not everyone who auditions the first time for a project is asked to return.

There are certain accepted practices for callbacks:

1. Wear the same clothes you wore to the first audition. You were called back because the production team liked your talent and your appearance sufficiently to warrant a second look. If you dress or fashion your hair differently you may look unfamiliar, or worse, entirely wrong to the production team and thus do yourself a disservice. In your appointment book mark down what you wear to every audition (and any other details about your appearance), so that when you go to the callback you can duplicate exactly how you looked the first time.

2. Bring the same two songs you sang the first time and sing the flashier, more exciting number first. Remind them of why they liked you the first time, and why they called you back.
3. The Directors may want to see you display colors other than the ones you showed previously. Thus it is imperative that you bring additional material with you—material you are rehearsed in and comfortable with. (Once again, your song portfolio can come in handy!) But don't ask them if they want you to do more! If they want to hear additional songs, they will request it of you.

As I wrote earlier in this book, if, when you are in the room, you are suddenly asked to do a certain type of song you have not prepared, for heaven's sake don't attempt to fumble through something you may only half-know. Don't ever try to perform when you are not ready. If you do, the last impression you leave with the production team will be one of sloppiness. If you have a parcel of songs to choose from and are still asked to something else, it is not bad form to say, "I'm sorry, I don't have anything like that under my belt. If you'd like, I could work up that kind of song and come in again." Most often, you will not have to learn anything new, although you may be asked to return for a second callback. If you do get a special request, try to get from the Director—or whoever is doing the asking—as specific an assignment as possible, so that when you return, you will be doing precisely what he thought he wanted.

A Touch of the Outrageous

I tremble a bit to include this topic for fear of its consequences. Throwing caution to the winds, I dutifully mention that some performers have gotten mileage out of their auditions by being slightly outrageous.

On television's *Tonight Show*, Director-Choreographer Tommy Tune *(Nine, My One and Only, Grand Hotel)* described to guest-hostess Joan Rivers how he auditioned in his performing days: While he sang the song "M-O-T-H-E-R"—"M is for the million things she gave me..."—he twisted his tall, lanky body to form the letters M-O-T-H-E-R. Ms. Rivers asked Mr. Tune if he would hire a person who came into an audition and did the same routine. Mr. Tune said yes, because it would show him that the actor had some imagination and a sense of humor.

In the 1950s a woman dancer entered the audition room on roller skates (perhaps echoing a famous Beatrice Lillie routine). She skated in, performed, and skated out. The footwear had nothing to do with her audition material, it was just to make her stand out from the crowd. Her ploy worked; she got jobs. (I can just hear the post-audition discussion: "Let's use the one on the roller skates...") I don't recommend this idea, because roller skates (or roller blades) won't allow you complete freedom of movement. But you know this already—from an earlier section of this book!

Two oft-told tales involve Mary Jo Catlett. Now well-known for her appearances in the 1980s on Raid commercials and for her role as Pearl on television's *Diff'rent Strokes,* Ms. Catlett had, by the time the first incident described below took place, already been on Broadway in *Hello, Dolly!* among other shows.

She, like many other performers, had a fear of auditioning—translation: fear of rejection—and it took her some time to conquer it. When she did, she too treated the audition as if she were performing a part in a play. Then it became great fun for her, and she went to just about any lengths to get a part—especially if she knew in advance something about the show.

In 1971, at the time her appointment was scheduled by the Casting Director for the Broadway musical *Diff'rent Strokes*—no relation to the similarly named television show—Ms. Catlett was asked to prepare a song and sing it as if hung over. After due consideration, she picked a song that would suggest the opposite of how one would feel in that condition: "I Feel Pretty" from *West Side Story*. In the audition room she put three chairs together, lay down on them on her back, and sang. After the first quatrain, she rolled over and fell flat on the floor and continued singing, facedown. She got the part.

Another story involving Ms. Catlett falls into the Chutzpa Department. For the Broadway revival of *The Pajama Game,* which was to be directed by the show's original Director, the late George Abbott, she auditioned for the part of the executive secretary, Mabel, and didn't hear anything after her audition. Through the grapevine she found out the producers were on the brink of hiring someone else but weren't enthusiastic about their choice. She got a call to go back and audition again as if she had never been there before. It was suggested that she wear a blonde wig—she is a brunette—and sing a different song; because if she did, in theory, Mr. Abbott would never know she was the same woman he wasn't interested in earlier. She took the suggestion and got the job, although she's convinced she didn't fool the ever-wise Mr. Abbott. P.S. She didn't have to wear the blonde wig in the show.

The funniest audition I ever witnessed was for *Trixie True, Teen Detective*. The Director asked everyone to bring a comedy number. Almost half of the men brought the song "Floozies" from *The Grass Harp*—an amusing song, but really not comic. One man, tall, rugged, and very masculine in a natural, self-assured way, had us all in stitches when he sang "I Enjoy Being A Girl" from *Flower Drum Song* in his rich baritone without any camping whatsoever.

Now these are examples of outrageous ideas which were successfully executed. I'm sure you can well imagine that for every one good idea there were dozens of misguided attempts. To cite but one example:

At an open call for *Into the Woods* during its Broadway run, a woman came in to audition wearing a frilly dress, totally inappropriate for her age and appearance. She was "50ish-but-thought-she-passed-for-30." Her choice of audition song was the 1934 Academy Award-winning "Continental," in what seemed to be a transcribed version of the entire (long!) movie arrangement. Fully choreographed. The lady sang. The lady danced. And during one of her dance sections she faced the Musical Director and lifted her skirt to reveal that she wasn't wearing any underclothing! The Musical Director's eyebrows appeared to shoot up to the ceiling and a huge shocked grin broke out on his face. Do you think the lady was cast? Not in this particular production.

In the "You-*Don't*-Gotta-Have-A-Gimmick" Department, you do not need a "gimmick" to succeed. Only talent. I just heard about a man who auditions singing a song to a puppet which he brings along with him. This is cute the first time people see it, but it gets stale pretty quickly. When he auditions for people a second time, they already know the puppet is coming and wish it weren't. The man uses this puppet all the time, and it's inappropriate in most situations. So if you want to do a "gimmick," make sure it relates to the show for which you are auditioning. Don't do it as your "standard" audition piece, and never do it in front of the same people twice.

If you can find a way to make yourself stand out by doing something extraordinarily different, do it. But please, first, whatever your idea is, try it out on several of your more conservative friends before you gamble at an audition. If you're at all in doubt as to the appropriateness of your plan, stick to something safe.

After the Audition

So now you've been conscientious, done all the preparation, and worked your tail off. You've also just done an audition and you feel, well, strange. Perhaps a little let down. It's natural. Perhaps your thoughts fall into one of the following categories:

1. I have no idea how it went.
2. I was terrible—they're never going to hire me.
3. I was terrific—but they didn't seem the least bit interested.
4. I was terrific—I'm sure I'm going to get cast.

Within reason, you should be able to tell how well you sang and/or danced, and how comfortable you felt as a performer, but that's about all. You cannot accurately measure the reactions of the production team. Even if they talked and ate sandwiches during your audition—which is rude on their part, but it's done—you shouldn't take that as a certain sign of a negative attitude towards you.

The only thing you should think after an audition is:

5. I gave a great audition. Even if I don't get cast I know they saw me at my best.

If you think your audition left room for improvement, try to figure out why so that you can correct the problem(s) next time.

Most importantly, if you think you did well but still didn't get cast, don't buy into thinking you are terrible or untalented. There are too many variables out of your control in an audition situation which include (but aren't limited to) the specific requirements of the show and the particular preferences of the creative team. You can't—and therefore shouldn't try to—second-guess what is on their minds as they listen to you. And if you have heard any "inside" information about what the production team has in mind from other actors, you should only listen with one ear: your actor colleagues constantly exchange misinformation and in this arena are not necessarily reliable sources.

Another factor most people are unaware of is that when currently running shows are looking for replacements, your skill and talent may not be the prime requirement: actors who fit the costumes and don't require transpositions can save a lot of money for the company (shades of Summer Stock!). Oh, you don't really believe me, do you? This kind of stuff doesn't happen on "Broadway!" Well, as Joan Rivers says, "Grow up!" Just recently, a currently running show replaced its leading man with a major, world-class star. His musical material was adjusted and transposed to suit him. But shortly before he joined the company the leading lady was replaced (with a wonderful performer who is not a star in the same class as her co-star). The Musical Director realized that she would sound better if her first number was to be transposed to a different key from the one the original actress used. The Producer denied the request—not because he didn't agree on artistic grounds, he just didn't want to spend the money! If you're up for a replacement in a show and are the wrong size or vocal range, you're probably out of luck regardless of your talent and preparation.

Unfortunately, it is simply not possible for you to get objective feedback on how your audition went. If you thought you did everything right and got cut early, or didn't get at least a callback, you probably will never know why. You were there to offer your talents to the production. If they didn't want your contribution, at least you tried. You should only concern yourself with taking charge of your own presentation and demonstrating your talent in the most satisfactory way possible. If you are consistently not getting hired, don't blame the world for not recognizing your true genius; the place to look is within yourself. You may be doing something wrong. And if this is the case, whatever you may be doing wrong can be corrected.

But human beings do not always behave predictably, or logically, and once in a great while one of the members of the production team may just have it in for you. In this case, your audition may be doomed before you start, as happened at the following audition:

Several years ago in New York City, all the people awaiting their turn to sing—about twenty—were invited to sit on little chairs on the stage to watch the other auditions. In the group was the girl-friend of one of the Producers. She had been flown in from Los Angeles by her producer-friend to try out, and was tastefully and becomingly attired in a black sheath with a strand of pearls around her neck. When her name was announced, she gave her music to the staff pianist and in a soprano voice sang "And This Is My Beloved." Beautifully. A nasty little voice from out front said, "Miss, you know that's not the right kind of song for our show. Do you have anything to belt?" Composed, she turned to the pianist and said, "I'll do 'Johnny One-Note'—start in D then move up to E-flat." And she told him at which point to modulate. She blew the roof off the the-atre. She was so terrific, in fact, that afterwards, everyone on stage spontaneously applauded her. Up from the audience came the man who had spoken earlier—the Director. On the stage, in front of everyone, he said "Miss, I know you're from the Coast, but first of all, your choice of material is terrible. You must never wear a black velvet sheath, and pearls are outclassed. Now tell me, what have you done before?" Summoning up all the dignity she could muster after that gratuitous humiliation, she said, "Well, in the beginning, I creat-ed heaven and earth."

Whatever your particular experience may be, always remember the words of the late Lehman Engel: "Rejection at an audition is not the conclusion of anything, only the end of a single exploration."

Audition for everything. The more you audition, the more expe-rience you get in actually doing an audition. And the more you're seen by people in the industry who could hire you for other shows. Casting Director Barry Moss explains, "Exposure to anybody in the industry is important. Be very careful how you treat people. The receptionist in the casting office today may be the head of casting for a television network tomorrow. Or even the conduit for that very moment. Everybody you meet is a little deposit in your safe-deposit box and may pay off later."

Keep plugging.

Stay confident.

Try new things.

If you have the talent, you'll get there.

APPENDIX A
A Partial List of Some of the Most Overdone, Uninspired, (and Inappropriate) Audition Songs

Use this list as a guide to songs you should not choose for your audition portfolio. It is current as of this writing. Songs go in and out of vogue, and one season lots of people will be doing the same song and, inexplicably, the next season no one will bring it in.

Take note that songs also appear here for more than just the reason that they are overdone. Songs such as the brilliant tour de force "Crossword Puzzle" and *Carousel's* magnificent "Soliloquy" are way too long to use as audition pieces. And songs such as "All That Jazz" and "Stars" don't reveal enough about the performer, no matter how well they are done.

Both types of songs should, as detailed in the main text in this book, not be considered ideal audition material.

Any song from *Jacques Brel*
Ain't Gonna Let You Break My Heart Again
All That Jazz *(Chicago)*
And This Is My Beloved *(Kismet)*
Anthem *(Chess)*
Anyone Can Whistle *(Anyone Can Whistle)*
Art Is Calling For Me *(The Enchantress)*
A Simple Song *(Mass)*
A Wonderful Guy *(South Pacific)*
Be A Lion *(The Wiz)*
Being Alive *(Company)*
Cabaret *(Cabaret)*
Can't Help Lovin' Dat Man *(Show Boat)*

Corner Of The Sky *(Pippin)*
Crossword Puzzle *(Starting Here, Starting Now)*
Don't Tell Mama *(Cabaret)*
Empty Chairs at Empty Tables *(Les Misérables)*
Everybody Says Don't *(Anyone Can Whistle)*
Everything's Coming Up Roses *(Gypsy)*
Extraordinary *(Pippin)*
Feelin' Good *(The Roar of the Greasepaint...)*
Funny *(City of Angels)*
Gethsemane *(Jesus Christ Superstar)*
Glitter And Be Gay (Candide)
God Bless The Child
Gorgeous *(The Apple Tree)*
Her Face *(Carnival)*
Hit Me With A Hot Note *(Sophisticated Ladies)*
I Can Cook Too *(On The Town)*
Ice Cream *(She Loves Me)*
I Could Have Been a Sailor
I Don't Remember Christmas *(Starting Here, Starting Now)*
If I Loved You *(Carousel)*
If I Sing *(Closer Than Ever)*
I Got Rhythm *(Girl Crazy)*
I'll Build A Stairway To Paradise *(George White's Scandals)*
I'll Never Fall In Love Again *(Promises, Promises)*
I Love A Piano *(Stop! Look! Listen!)*
I Met A Girl *(Bells Are Ringing)*
It Never Entered My Mind *(Higher and Higher)*
I Wish I Were In Love Again *(Babes In Arms)*
Joey, Joey, Joey *(The Most Happy Fella)*
Johnny One-Note *(Babes In Arms)*
Keepin' Out of Mischief Now *(Ain't Misbehavin')*
Losing My Mind *(Follies)*
Love, I Hear *(A Funny Thing Happened On The Way To The Forum)*
Love, Look Away *(110 in the Shade)*
Luck Be A Lady *(Guys and Dolls)*
Mama, A Rainbow *(Minnie's Boys)*
Maria *(West Side Story)*

Marry Me a Little *(Company)*
Maybe *(Annie)*
Maybe This Time *(Cabaret—movie)*
Metaphor *(The Fantasticks)*
Moonfall *(The Mystery of Edwin Drood)*
Much More *(The Fantasticks)*
My Ship *(Lady in the Dark)*
Never *(On The Twentieth Century)*
Nobody Does It Like Me *(Seesaw)*
Not a Day Goes By *(Merrily We Roll Along)*
Not Since Ninevah *(Kismet)*
Nothing *(A Chorus Line)*
On My Own *(Fame—movie)*
On The Other Side Of The Tracks *(Little Me)*
People *(Funny Girl)*
Promises, Promises *(Promises, Promises)*
She Loves Me *(She Loves Me)*
Soliloquy *(Carousel)*
Someone to Watch Over Me *(Oh, Kay!, Crazy For You)*
Stars *(Les Misérables)*
Stranger In Paradise *(Kismet)*
Strong Woman Number *(I'm Getting My Act Together ...)*
The Greatest Love Of All *(The Greatest—movie)*
The Impossible Dream *(Man of La Mancha)*
The Joker *(The Roar of the Greasepaint...)*
There's Always One You Can't Forget *(Dance a Little Closer)*
They Call The Wind Maria *(Paint Your Wagon)*
They Were You *(The Fantasticks)*
Think of Me *(The Phantom of the Opera)*
Tomorrow *(Annie)*
Tonight At Eight *(She Loves Me)*
Try Me *(She Loves Me)*
Wait Till You See Her *(By Jupiter)*
What Am I Doin'? *(Closer Than Ever)*
What I Did For Love *(A Chorus Line)*
Where Am I Going? *(Sweet Charity)*
Why Can't I Walk Away? *(Maggie Flynn)*

You Can Always Count on Me *(City of Angels)*
You're Nothing Without Me *(City of Angels)*
Your Feet's Too Big *(Ain't Misbehavin')*

It's also a good idea to avoid brand new hit songs. Even before *Cats* opened on Broadway too many singers performed "Memory" at auditions, each one thinking that they would be the only one to be doing it at that point in time. (*Cats* opened in London a year and a half before it came to New York.) And avoid "rediscovered" songs from currently playing revivals. No sooner did the 1994 revival of *Damn Yankees* open on Broadway then "Whatever Lola Wants" enjoyed an immediate resurgence of popularity as an audition song. It's too obvious a choice. Play it safer with little-known older material. There's tons of it to choose from!

APPENDIX B
Your Photo and Resumé

Until that pie-in-the-sky day arrives when you achieve stardom, you will need to have current pictures and up-to-date résumés ready to give to anyone who may cast you in anything. So, as promised earlier, here are a few observations on that ubiquitous duo. Note to newcomers: The trade papers are full of ads for photographers and for résumé-typing services. If one has not been recommended to you, shop around, compare prices and quality of work. Then, if you have to, draw straws and pick one.

Your picture and résumé must be attached. There's nothing that looks more unprofessional than carrying them around unattached. Spend a few minutes at home pasting the résumés to the backs of the photographs, using rubber cement. This advice is so basic, and so ignored, that I have recently seen written in audition announcements "Please attach photo and résumé."

Don't present a packet of reviews and clippings at an audition. The people evaluating the auditions don't have time to read them— neither when you are in the room nor later on. Nor are they the least bit interested in doing so. All the great things that have been said about you in print will do no earthly good if you make a poor showing in person.

Keep your résumé to one page. If you have so many credits that it takes more than one page to list them all, just put the most important ones down. Or make up two separate résumés, each geared to different types of work, i.e., one that lists all your commercials and industrial shows.

Don't make the résumé too cluttered. You want your experience to be immediately comprehensible. In this regard, always list your most important credits first. Use this order as a guideline for your musical résumé:

1. Broadway productions
2. National tours
3. Stock, regional, and dinner theatre productions
4. College productions
5. Film and television shows
6. Skills

Be factual. I remember one particular actor who listed he had worked for a particular Director. Unfortunately, he was auditioning that day for the Director named—and the Director was certain that he had never worked with that actor. My point is: Don't fabricate credits. If you're worried that your résumé looks unimpressive, don't worry. If you're talented, your credits will grow quickly enough.

An American performer's résumé stated that he was adept at a British accent. The Director, a native of the British isles, queried the actor, "You can do a British accent?" The actor replied "Yes, I worked for a British mime troupe."

Never put any unnecessary information on the résumé. At an audition I played at some years ago, an actress presented her résumé, and after her less-than-impressive audition it was immediately consigned to the trash basket. I retrieved it, kept it, and still have it in my files because it is so bizarre. On it was written: "My most exciting experience was natural childbirth. However, it's hardly marketable."

> One performer had this on his résumé:
> "Did voice-overs for films for the deaf."

I have often wondered why so many people put on their résumés, under "Skills," that they can drive a car? When was the last time you heard of anyone in a stage musical needing to drive a real car on-stage? I rest my case.

As for your photo, make sure it is recent and that it looks like you. Of course you always want a flattering photograph, but it is important that your picture resemble the person standing in front of those casting the show. After you leave the room, your photo is all they have to remember you by. The picture must call to mind the actor the casting people just saw.

A surprising number of women have had composite photo résumés done containing pictures of themselves in the nude. This is certainly an attention-getting device and it does work. The résumés do stand out from the others and are often kept by the male members of the production team. They are also frequently tacked up on office walls. But the ladies are never seriously considered for roles. Unless, maybe, for *Oh, Calcutta!*

APPENDIX C
To Agent or not to Agent (And Other Questions Answered)

As I mentioned earlier, it is difficult to secure an audition for a principle role in a Broadway show unless you are recommended by a reputable theatrical agent. So how do you go about getting an agent to represent you? I posed this and other questions to Jeffrey Dunn, a New York based Casting Director, when he was an agent in the Musical Theatre department of the Fifi Oscard agency. (What follows is a modified version of that interview.)

When Mr. Dunn and I spoke, Actors' Equity (the union to which all professional theatre performers must belong) rulings made it extraordinarily hard for non-Equity performers to be auditioned for any productions having a contract with that union. This encompasses all Broadway shows, Off-Broadway shows, national touring companies, bus and truck tours, and most professional companies across the nation. After June 1, 1988 the ruling changed, and all performers who satisfy certain criteria, whether members of Equity or not, can be seen and considered.

QUESTION: *But aren't your chances of getting cast better if you are a full-fledged member of Equity?*

JEFFREY DUNN: If you've just arrived in town, I don't think the best idea is to get your Equity card immediately. Unless you're interested in being a chorus person for the rest of your life, you're better off getting roles under your belt in good non-Equity stock companies. If you're talented, it's quite possible you can get some really good parts that you wouldn't get in an Equity company for years. It's also a way to start making contacts and connections. Quite frequently the Directors at those theatres do move into better things. The Second-Assistant Stage Manager of this year's dinner-theatre production could be directing a Broadway show in five years.

Q: *Where does someone find out about these theatres?*

JD: There's a book published called *Summer Theatre Directory,* edited by Jill Charles. From interviews with people who have worked in them, the book discusses all the stock theatres; what the pay scale is like; what the living conditions are; whether people enjoy working there, etc. It's important to know this ahead of time, because when you're talking about non-Equity you're not covered by any rulings except public health, and that sometimes comes into play at some of these theatres.

Q: *So how long should a performer continue to do non-Equity work before he gets his Equity card?*

JD: Remember that once you get your card, you can never act in a professional non-Equity production again without Equity's express permission. I know many young actors who, having finished a successful season of stock—doing nine musicals in nine weeks—think, "Now I'm ready! I want my Equity card!" They somehow get it within about a year and never get another Equity job again. Many promising careers grind to a halt as a result of getting the card. I see people all the time who come to me with résumés with one Equity credit and the rest is all nonunion, and not recent nonunion work at that, and I can't do a lot with them because they're competing with everybody who has ever been in a Broadway show or national tour. I think you should always be functioning on the level where you're competitive. Those who attend non-Equity open calls for Broadway shows and are not getting the jobs think, "All I need is to get my card and then I'll work." Do they really think that if they go to the same calls and compete with the Equity people they're going to get cast? That the letters A.E.A next to their names will make them sound better? It won't. If you need an Equity card, you'll get it—and I've rarely seen somebody not get it when he was ready. But I've seen many people who got it when they weren't.

Q: *When should performers get an agent?*

JD: Again, when they're ready. An agent tends to work in the more important venues, the ones that are going to be income-producing or career-building. An agent is not going to be that interested in booking you for a summer in New Hampshire—making minimum, doing interesting shows every week—or putting you in an Off-Broadway musical, unless it seems to have the potential to move somewhere. There are many people who come to me who are very talented, but whom I don't think I can do a lot with yet because they are just so green. They don't have the experience. I'm reluctant to take on somebody that I can't get seen. Even with people who've been on Broadway—assuming that their agents have good reputations and good credibility—if Casting Directors don't know the actor's work it is sometimes difficult to get them seen for every project—or even for the ones they are right for. Be sure when you go after an agent that you have something to offer him other than just your talent. You have to have credentials that you were able to get on your own. Start looking as soon as you feel your talent is at a level where you can utilize an agent, but don't expect to be a signed client until agents are going to be able to keep you busy working. An agent is happiest when his clients are working.

It's never a bad thing at any point in your career to send a picture and résumé to an agent with a note saying, "I'm not represented right now. Perhaps if you're interested, we can talk." Don't be crestfallen if they won't see you initially. And then if they'll meet with you but won't do anything for you, just keep in touch with them; let them know when you're doing things, and gradually, if they see that your career seems to be moving, they will jump on the bandwagon quickly. They'd be foolish not to. But when you first get to town, it's just important to work, because work begets work.

Q: *Obviously, if an actor is working, he's also being seen and exposed to others in the business.*

JD: Also, the people you meet and work with form a network where you exchange information. Although not always 100 percent reliable, it's a start in learning which Director is good and which isn't; which agent is good and which isn't; whom you can trust, whom you can't; don't work at this theatre, and so on. From working, people know you. Even if they just see your name in a program, it's better than not. Your name should get to be familiar to people. But you shouldn't work in stuff that's not good. It's very possible to take mediocre material and make it wonderful, as many Tony Award winners who've been in mediocre musicals would bear out. But don't be involved in something that you would be embarrassed to invite people to. As important as it is to keep working, it's also important to keep an eye on the long term—that you're looking to build a career. Certainly don't invite an agent to a show if you're the only good thing in it; don't make them spend an evening seeing a rotten show for your terrific five minutes. Better to drop them a note and say, "I'm doing this show and I think I'm very good in it, however, I don't think the rest of it is that good. If you're really interested in seeing me, come between 9:30-10:00, that's when I do my stuff." It's unlikely that the agent will come, but the fact that you had that much faith in your work and were considerate of the agent at the same time will not go unnoticed.

Q: *Do agents scour the town going to showcases and the like looking for new talent?*

JD: As with any group of people, you can't generalize. I do go out a lot to cover people for the areas I work in. However, one of the areas I work in is musicals. So I don't miss an important musical project anywhere.

Q: *Do you approach people you like in shows to see if they're represented?*

JD: Yes, definitely. If they say they're not represented, then I give them my card and tell them to call. And do you want to hear something amazing? Quite frequently they don't. Maybe they're afraid to call or they wonder if I really meant it. I don't give out my card if I don't want to hear from them, even at the risk of hurting somebody's feelings, which I hate to do, but I really won't lead people on. If you do good work and people see it, and they think that you have a big career, they're going to go up and talk to you afterwards. I think most agents would.

Q: *Okay, you're an actor, and a agent has asked to see you. Should you sign with the agent?*

JD: With some agents, the minute they meet you they want to sign you. You have to find the right agent. Signing with an agent is like a marriage. It's a relationship. You have to have good communication. I don't think that can happen in a fifteen minute meeting; it can only happen in time. And it takes two for it to work well. For the agent, he needs to be sure that he can get you seen, that he can keep you busy. And you have to find out whether you're going to be submitted for things that you're right for and for the kinds of things you want to be doing. You can have a somewhat successful career without being signed by an agent. There are several people who have had Broadway careers but who, for one reason or another, are unsigned. Getting signed means finding an agent who knows what you do, likes what you do, and knows what to do with it. And that doesn't always happen. However, when you get to a certain point, you've got to have an agent or a manager, at least to do your contract negotiating.

Q: *Any more general advice?*

JD: You have to have the confidence in your own talent and your own ability—to know you're going to hit it, but to keep working on it and nurturing it like any growing thing. And the patience to put up with everything you have to put up with until that time comes without going crazy. You have to find things that you can do to keep yourself from getting nuts.

Q: *Like what?*

JD: Like getting together with actors and spending an evening reading a play. Going to the Lincoln Center Library every two weeks and taking out albums of two musicals you never heard before. Getting together with a friend who plays the piano—and maybe even a bunch of friends—and just singing through music. Going to the movie musicals that play the revival houses. Buying standing room for a Broadway show that you've seen already and seeing what has happened to it six months later, or seeing how the replacements are doing. I learned a great deal when I would go to shows many times and see replacements and see how many different ways there are to approach a character. To see every single lady play Dolly was very instructive. There's no one way. When I sold orange drinks at the Shubert Theatre when *Promises, Promises* was playing, I saw over a long period of time what can happen to the performances. Jerry Orbach was able to keep his performance absolutely fresh every night; other people were not quite as good at it. To see where the laughs came with different houses. To keep learning and growing is so important. That's what you do in between jobs. Just because nobody's paying you to work doesn't mean you stop working. Go to dance classes. Do those auditions. Try to keep yourself happy. Because if you're depressed and you go into an audition depressed, it's going to show. Nobody wants to hire anyone who's desperate.

At the end of *The Count of Monte Cristo* by Alexandre Dumas is a wonderful quote, which reads:

> The Count just told us that all human wisdom was contained in these two words: wait and hope.

Show business is a lot like that.

APPENDIX D
Helpful Names and Addresses

The first—and best—place to look for names and addresses of book, record, and sheet-music stores is in your local Yellow Pages under the headings "Book Dlrs.," Records, Tapes, and Discs– Retail," and "Sheet Music," respectively. Professional music copyists can either be found through your city's local chapter of the musician's union—American Federation of Musicians—or through the music department of a university. Pianists can be located through the latter as well. The musician's union cannot recommend a certain music copyist over another, but they can provide you with a list of those available in your area.

In cities with a substantial theatrical industry, such as New York, Los Angeles, and London, there are a number of related businesses prepared to serve the trade knowledgeably. What follows is a workable but incomplete listing of some of the more established firms that you could contact for assistance by phone, mail, or if it is a retail store, in person.

SHEET MUSIC—NEW YORK CITY

Colony Music
1619 Broadway
New York, NY 10019
(212) 265-2050
> They stock a large selection of out-of-print sheet music and occasionally have some out-of-print oddities. They also have a huge selection of recordings, both in-print and out-of-print.

Music Exchange
151 West 46 Street
New York, NY 10036
(212) 354-5858
    They stock a large selection of out-of-print sheet music.

Performing Arts Library
Lincoln Center Plaza
New York, NY 10023

SHEET MUSIC—LOS ANGELES

Hollywood Sheet Music
7777 Sunset Blvd
Los Angeles, CA 90046
(213) 850-1075

RECORDS, TAPES, AND DISCS—NEW YORK CITY

Footlight Records
113 East 12th Street
New York, NY 10003
(212) 533-1572

Ben Bagley's Discs:
Painted Smiles Records
74-09 37th Avenue
Suite 420
Jackson Heights, NY 11372
(718) 898-6964

Music Masters
Box Office Recordings
PO Box 2240
Stamford, CT 06906-0240
(203) 328-0094

Shadowland-Rialto Recordings
(distributed nationally by:)
Records Ltd.
P.O. Box 20136
Los Angeles, CA 90006

Tower Records
2107 Broadway
New York, NY 10023
(212) 799-2500
> Maintains a very complete selection of in-print compact
> discs and cassettes in this and their other locations.

RECORDS, TAPES, AND DISCS—LOS ANGELES

Tower Records
8801 Sunset Blvd
West Hollywood, CA 90069
(310) 657-7300
> Maintains a very complete selection of in-print compact
> discs and cassettes in this and their other locations.

RECORDS, TAPES, DISCS AND THEATRE BOOKS
—LONDON

Dress Circle
57-59 Monmouth Street
Upper St. Martins Lane
London WC2H 9DG
(0171) 240-2227

BOOKSTORES—NEW YORK CITY

Earlier in this book I mentioned the importance of becoming familiar with the standard repertory of the music theatre. Many musicals have had their scripts published and are therefore available to read and study. First, try your local library. Then, try the following bookstores—again, an incomplete list:

Barnes & Noble
    (all stores)

B. Dalton
    (all stores)

Coliseum Books
1771 Broadway
New York, NY 10019
(212) 757-8381

Drama Book Shop
723 Seventh Avenue
New York, NY 10019
(212) 944-0595

Scribners
    (all stores)

Shakespeare and Co. Downtown
Shakespeare and Co. Uptown
2259 Broadway
New York, NY 10024
(212) 580-7800

BOOKSTORES—LOS ANGELES AND SAN FRANCISCO

Barnes & Noble
(all stores)

Drama Books
134 9th Street
San Francisco, CA 94103
(415) 255-0604

Limelight Books
1803 Market Street
San Francisco, CA 94103
(415) 864-2265

Samuel French
7623 Sunset Boulevard
Hollywood, CA 90046
(213) 876-0570

BOOKSTORES—BOSTON AND CAMBRIDGE

Baker's Plays
100 Chauncy Street
Boston, MA 02111
(617) 482-1280

Barnes & Noble
(all stores)

Wordsworth
30 Brattle Street
Cambridge, MA 02138
(617) 354-5201

BOOKSTORES—CHICAGO

Act I
2632 North Mineola Street
Chicago, IL 60614
(312) 348-6757

Borders
    (all stores)

Scenes
3168 North Clark Street
Chicago, IL 60657
(312) 525-1007

BOOKSTORES—SEATTLE

Borders
    (all stores)

Elliot Bay Bookstore
101 South Main Street
Seattle, WA 98104
(206) 624-6600

The Play's the Thing
514 East Pike Capitol Hill
Seattle, WA 98122
(206) 322-7529

BOOKSTORES—TORONTO

Theatrebooks
11 St. Thomas Street
Toronto
Ontario, Canada M5F 2B7

BOOKSTORES—WASHINGTON, DC

Backstage
2101-P Street NW
Wahington, DC 20037

BOOKSTORES—LONDON

Dillons
1 Malet Street
London WC1E 7JB

W & G Foyles Ltd.
113-119 Charing Cross Road
London WV2H OEB

National Theatre Book Shop
Upper Ground South Bank
London, England SEI 9PX

Off-StageTheatre Book Shop
37 Chalk Farm Road
London, England NW1 8AJ

Samuel French
52 Fitzroy Street
London W1P 6JR
England

Waterstone's
    (all stores)

MUSIC PREPARATION & SUPPLIES—NEW YORK CITY

Associated Music—Copy Service
333 West 52 Street
New York, NY 10019
(212) 265-2400
> Duplicating services provided, as well as music paper and supplies.

Chelsea Music Service, Inc.
311 West 43 Street
Suite 1407
New York, NY 10036
(212) 541-8656
> Copyists and music reproduction service provided.

King Brand Music Papers
250 West 49 Street
New York, NY 10019
(212) 246-0488
> Provides music reproduction service, as well as music paper and supplies.

MUSIC PREPARATION AND SUPPLIES—LOS ANGELES

Bob Bornstein
Music Library
Paramount Studios
5451 Marathon
Hollywood, CA 90038
(213) 956-5905
> Provides copyist services.

Judy Green Music
1616 Cahuenga Boulevard
Hollywood, CA 90028
(213) 466-2491
  Provides music reproduction service, as well as music paper
  and supplies.

Bill Hughes
10908 Riverside Drive
North Hollywood, CA 91602
(818) 508-8001
  Provides copyist services.

JoAnn Kane Music Service
2440 South Sepulveda Blvd
Suite 118
Los Angeles, CA 90064
(310) 231-9733
  Provides copyist services.

Valle Music Reproduction
12441 Riverside Drive
Hollywood, CA 91607
(818) 762-0615
  Provides music reproduction service, as well as music paper
  and supplies.

LAGNIAPPE
One Last Audition Story

A woman showed up at the casting call for every show Noël Coward did—musicals, straight plays, and revues. She always appeared well dressed, but her singing left lots to be desired. After many years, Mr. Coward, in deference to her tenacity rather than her talent, stepped up to the edge of the stage and said, "I'm very happy to tell you that at last we have a part for you." "Oh, no, Mr. Coward," she said, "I don't take parts. I just audition." And she grandly swept out.

DONALD OLIVER, a native New Yorker, compiled and edited two previous books: the acclaimed collection of George S. Kaufman's writings entitled *By George,* and *The Greatest Revue Sketches.* He contributed articles to New York's *Playbill* magazine and reviewed computer games regularly for a leading computer periodical.

As a composer, he studied at the Manhattan School of Music and was part of the BMI Musical Theatre Workshop under the direction of the late Lehman Engel. He wrote the score for the musical, *The Case of the Dead Flamingo Dancer,* in collaboration with author/lyricist Dan Butler, which was produced both in the United States and in England.

Since 1978 he has worked with Chelsea Music Service, Inc. in preparing the music for the Broadway productions of *Assassins, Cats, Five Guys Named Moe, Guys and Dolls, Into The Woods, Jerome Robbins' Broadway, Kiss of the Spider Woman, La Cage aux Folles, Merrily We Roll Along, Passion, ShowBoat, Starlight Express, State Fair, Sugar Babies, Sunset Boulevard, The Phantom of the Opera, The Secret Garden,* and *The Who's TOMMY,* among countless other shows, films, club acts, and recordings.

As Artistic Director for the Octagon Theatre Company in New York, he co-produced well-received revivals of *Knickerbocker Holiday, Zorba,* and *Drat! The Cat!*

His favorite job was playing pit piano for *Gypsy* with Angela Lansbury and he can be heard playing the celesta on a recording of lullabies, "All Through The Night", sung by opera diva Marilyn Horne.

Smith and Kraus *Books For Actors*
THE MONOLOGUE SERIES
The Best Men's / Women's Stage Monologues of 1994
The Best Men's / Women's Stage Monologues of 1993
The Best Men's / Women's Stage Monologues of 1992
The Best Men's / Women's Stage Monologues of 1991
The Best Men's / Women's Stage Monologues of 1990
One Hundred Men's / Women's Stage Monologues from the 1980's
2 Minutes and Under: Original Character Monologues for Actors
Street Talk: Original Character Monologues for Actors
Uptown: Original Character Monologues for Actors
Ice Babies in Oz: Original Character Monologues for Actors
Monologues from Contemporary Literature: Volume I
Monologues from Classic Plays
100 Great Monologues from the Renaissance Theatre
100 Great Monologues from the Neo-Classical Theatre
100 Great Monologues from the 19th C. Romantic and Realistic Theatres

YOUNG ACTORS SERIES
Great Scenes and Monologues for Children
New Plays from A.C.T.'s Young Conservatory
Great Scenes for Young Actors from the Stage
Great Monologues for Young Actors
Multicultural Monologues for Young Actors
Multicultural Scenes for Young Actors

CONTEMPORARY PLAYWRIGHTS SERIES
Romulus Linney: 17 Short Plays
Eric Overmyer: Collected Plays
Lanford Wilson: 21 Short Plays
William Mastrosimone: Collected Plays
Horton Foote: 4 New Plays
Israel Horovitz: 16 Short Plays
Israel Horovitz Vol. II: New England Blue
Terrence McNally: 15 Short Plays
Humana Festival '93: The Complete Plays
Humana Festival '94: The Complete Plays
Humana Festival '95: The Complete Plays
Women Playwrights: The Best Plays of 1992
Women Playwrights: The Best Plays of 1993
Women Playwrights: The Best Plays of 1994
EST Marathon '94: One-Act Plays
EST Marathon '95: One-Act Plays
Showtime's Act One Festival '95: One-Act Plays

CAREER DEVELOPMENT SERIES
The Great Acting Teachers and Their Methods
Nikos Psacharopoulos: The Master Class
Taken To The Stage: An Autobiography by Mimi Kennedy
The Job Book II: 100 Day Jobs for Actors
The Job Book: 100 Acting Jobs for Actors
The Smith and Kraus Monologue Index
The Actor's Guide to Qualified Coaches: New York
The Actor's Guide to Qualified Coaches: LA
What to Give Your Agent for Christmas and 100 Other Tips for the Working Actor
The Camera Smart Actor
The Sanford Meisner Approach
Anne Bogart: Viewpoints
The Actor's Chekhov
Kiss and Tell: Restoration Scenes, Monologues, & History
Cold Readings: Some Do's and Don'ts for Actors at Auditions

If you require pre-publication information about upcoming Smith and Kraus books, you may receive our semi-annual catalogue, free of charge, by sending your name and address to *Smith and Kraus Catalogue, P.O. Box 127, One Main Street, Lyme, NH 03768. Or call us at (800) 895-4331, fax (603) 795-4427.*